It must be nearly impo
(reliable, proven, full-c
be anything but search
how I found this book to be and that's how I'm sure it will be for you
too. I thank God for David and this 'conversation' he has given us on
the task that is key to the future of the church.

SIMON MANCHESTER
Senior Mentor of the John Chapman Preaching Initiative,
Moore College, Sydney

Having known David Jackman for many years, profited from his
preaching ministry and shared with him in ministry partnership in a
local church, I eagerly looked forward to reading this book. It reads
like the collected thoughts and wisdom which are the fruit of fifty
years of preaching ministry. I see it as not just a book to be read once
but a resource to dip in to time and time again for encouragement
and correction. Perhaps best of all I found in myself a fresh vision and
enthusiasm for preaching ministry as I was reminded of the ultimate
purpose of preaching, which is to present people mature in Christ.

MIKE NEVILLE
Vicar, St Simon Zelotes, London

This is vintage Jackman! Here is a wealth of perceptive Biblical and
pastoral advice and encouragement to preachers. It includes helpful
reminders of the need for expository preaching, and also clarifying
warnings of some of the traps that expository preachers fall into.
These are mostly when useful servants become damaging masters,
for example when extensive exegesis overwhelms the sermon, or when
Biblical Theology or Systematic Theology obliterate the Bible passage.
I found the chapters on preaching law and liberty and on preaching
for maturity especially helpful. The greatest strength of the book is its
focus on transformational preaching. Thankyou David!

PETER ADAM
Vicar Emeritus, St Jude's Church, Carlton, Victoria, Australia

I've loved reading David's reflections 'over a coffee' as he suggests. And,
in truth, it has been so much more than that. This book is full of
refreshing wisdom that is so useful and hugely relevant to my ministry.
I have highlighted vast swathes of it and have already found myself
putting many ideas into practice. I will keep returning to this book
and sharing it over many years to come.

DAVID SECKINGTON
Assistant pastor, Trinity Church, London

'Preaching that is balanced and well crafted', one chapter title in this book, surely sums up what David Jackman has embodied over half a century in his own ministry in the UK and around the world. This book draws together a host of themes and vital questions for preachers and would-be preachers, addressing them with the thoroughgoing biblical understanding and deep pastoral wisdom so many of us admire in David. His long and remarkable service, both as a preacher and teacher and as a trainer of others, means there are few whose insights are so valuable to those who would follow him in this task.

WILLIAM J. U. PHILIP
Senior Minister, The Tron Church, Glasgow

Transforming Preaching

Reflecting on 50 years of of Word-Ministry

David Jackman

PT RESOURCES

CHRISTIAN
FOCUS

Copyright © Proclamation Trust Media 2021

Paperback ISBN: 978-1-5271-0692-5
Ebook ISBN: 978-1-5271-0780-9

10 9 8 7 6 5 4 3 2 1

Published in 2021
by
Christian Focus Publications Ltd.,
Geanies House, Fearn, Ross-shire,
IV20 1TW, Scotland, Great Britain
www.christianfocus.com
with
Proclamation Trust Resources,
Willcox House, 140-148 Borough High Street,
London, SE1 1LB, England, Great Britain.
www.proctrust.org.uk

Cover design by Moose77.com

Printed and bound by
Bell & Bain, Glasgow

Contents

ACKNOWLEDGEMENTS

I would like to thank Heather, my dear wife of fifty years, for her constant encouragement to me in my ministry and for her patient support during the hours of 'retirement' which have gone into writing this book. She has done more for me and means more to me than I can ever adequately express.

Thanks are also due to all the colleagues with whom I have worked over the years, including the many saints who are now 'present with the Lord', but whose dedicated service in preaching and writing have been such a blessing and stimulating example to me. Among current friends, I have particularly valued conversations I have had with Mike Neville, Charlie Thomson, Albert Yu, Charles Malton, Malcolm Riley, Dave Seckington, Todd Kelly, Tim Sattler, Peter Nicholas, Carrie Sandom, Willie Philip and Jon Gemmell—to name a few—on different aspects of the book.

My warmest thanks are due to Nancy Olsen, who has deciphered the calligraphy and typed my hand-written manuscript with such patience and precision and whose secretarial expertise has been such a help to me over the past twenty years. Finally, I wish to express my appreciation to the Christian Focus publishing team, who have seen the manuscript through to its publication. Christian team-work is a wonderful thing and I have been the beneficiary of so many kindnesses and so much hard work by many dedicated colleagues and friends, for which I thank both them and the Lord whom they serve.

D.J.J.

SERIES PREFACE

The Proclamation Trust's *Practical Preaching* series of books is written in order to explore the culture and context of preaching God's Word. It is different from our *Teaching the Bible* series which offers help in understanding and teaching books of the Bible. Instead these books look at wider issues and aspects of the task of preaching and teaching God's Word. Previous volumes have included, *Hearing the Spirit, Burning Hearts, The Priority of Preaching & Bible Delight.*

In this volume, David Jackman, reflecting on over fifty years of Word-ministry offers real encouragement and help with some of the ongoing challenges and pitfalls facing the preacher. Each chapter addresses a different theme that will shape and sharpen the reader in their thinking about what it means to be a faithful expositor and servant of the Word.

David Jackman is the ideal person to write a book like this. David has been preaching and training preachers longer than many of us have been alive. He is a terrific encourager of preachers and his insights, observations and exhortations will provide great stimulus for your own thinking. The referenced works are a treasure trove all of their own and taking time to do further reading will only multiply the benefit. I strongly recommend sitting down with a cup of coffee and this book and gleaning from the wisdom distilled in these pages.

May the fruit of time spent in this book be transforming preaching, as by God's grace you grow and develop in this most difficult and blessed endeavour.

As ever we are very thankful for Christian Focus and their ongoing partnership in our book publishing ministry. Without their passion, enthusiasm, patience and expertise these books would never see the light of day.

Jonathan Gemmell
London
2020

Author's Preface

It has been my privilege to be actively involved in teaching God's Word for over fifty years. My ministry began in 1968 in the student world, working for the Inter-Varsity Fellowship (now known as UCCF) and then, after theological studies, for fifteen years as a local church minister at Above Bar Church in the centre of the city of Southampton. This was followed by an invitation from the Proclamation Trust to found and direct the Cornhill Training Course in London, which focuses on providing basic tools and practical experience in communicating the Bible, for potential preachers and teachers. When appointed President of the Proclamation Trust, my role then broadened into preaching workshops and ministry conferences for ministers and trainees, both in the UK and further afield, which continues to be the major focus of my ministry in 'retirement'. Throughout this time I have also had the privilege of preaching regularly in local churches, in many locations, but primarily over the last thirty years at St Helen's, Bishopsgate, and St Simon Zelotes, Chelsea, for which I have been extremely grateful.

During those fifty years the world has changed in so many ways, almost beyond recognition, as has church life in all its variety of expression, theological and denominational. Rapid change is perhaps the only constant factor of 21st century life. Yet beneath the superficial differences, the unchanging realities of human need and God's rescue mission, through the gospel, remain the same. What else remains the same is the challenge to each generation of Bible teachers, indeed to everyone who seeks to communicate God's truth, whatever the occasion, which focuses on what to teach and how to communicate it. For some time now I have felt that it might be useful to share some of my personal reflections from my life-time in Biblical ministry, mainly as an encouragement and stimulus to those who are seeking to continue faithfully in the task, not to grow weary in well-doing. But I hope it might also be useful to a younger generation who are setting out on the adventure of a life-time dedicated to the ministry of God's Word. It is in that spirit that what follows is offered.

I want to make it clear that this is not a 'how to' book. It does not deal with the basics of Biblical interpretation, or talk preparation, or many of the practical issues involved in expository teaching. This is necessary material, which I have tried to cover in my set of instruction videos, with practical examples and exercises, which constitute the series, 'Equipped to Preach the Word', downloadable free of charge from the Proclamation Trust website, www.proctrust.org.uk/equipped.

I hope this book is more like a conversation over a cup of coffee in its approach, sharing some of the things I think I have learned. I know very well how demanding the task is

and how difficult the times are to be a consistently faithful
Bible teacher, an unashamed worker 'who rightly handles the
word of truth'. This is the most privileged of opportunities,
but calls for great diligence and hard work. All of us who
teach need the encouragement of others to keep on working
at our calling and I am particularly thankful to those who
have supported me down the years, with their advice,
encouragement, critiques and fellowship in prayer, which
mean that I have never felt isolated. I think I can honestly
say that I have never gone into a pulpit unprepared, but I
have often come out of it disappointed and discouraged by
my own failure or inability. I have learned, however, that I
am likely to be the worst judge of my effectiveness and that
it is not a very profitable activity to attempt. As the old
hymn puts it, 'Leave God to order all thy ways and trust
in him whate'er betide'. But it can be helpful to hear from
someone who has a few more miles on the clock and to
whom the journey may be a bit more familiar.

Much of what follows is as much about living the Christian
life as teaching it. It is as much about the transforming life
of the preacher and the congregation as it is about the task
of preaching. This must be right because the two have to be
integrated if we are to be authentic in our proclamation of
God's truth. It will not reach the hearers' hearts if it has not
first been at work in the preacher's heart. As John Chapman
used to say, 'Just because you're a minister doesn't let you off
being a Christian!' Throughout these chapters I have tried
to reference the expository work, on which my convictions
are founded, and to show my own working as succinctly
as possible. I have also included numerous quotations and
ideas from other writers who have helped shape my thinking

over the years. Some of these go back a long way, but I find
their wisdom still powerful and helpful, which is perhaps a
reminder that not everything good and beneficial has to be
new. Over the years I have tried to read widely on theological
and ministry issues, and I have found great stimulus
in accessing the wide and growing range of evangelical
scholarship. For me it has been a channel of instruction
and challenge, but also of spiritual refreshment to have a
more 'heavyweight' book on the go. The only problem now
is trying to keep up with the avalanche of material available,
but I hope that some of the authors I have quoted may be
able to help you, if you delve deeper into their books.

I am aware, of course, that some of what I say challenges
some of the 'shibboleths' of contemporary evangelical
attitudes, but my hope is that you will see these comments
and questions as an invitation to consider again your own
position on the issues raised. My intention is not to be
negatively critical, but to encourage thought and debate
about how we all might develop and improve our ability to
communicate God's unchanging truth in our confused and
confusing times. I am indebted to my friend and mentor,
Dick Lucas, for his teaching, example and penetrating
questions over many years and not least for his persistent
encouragement to put pen to paper during the 'lockdown'
and so to 'get the book written'. May God raise up across the
world-wide church a whole new generation of 'unashamed
workers', to His glory and praise.

DAVID JACKMAN.
Eastbourne.
September 2020

1.

Preaching with the right goal in view

As the apostle Paul reflects on his life and ministry, in chains as a Roman prisoner, he writes to the Christians in Colossae one of the most revealing paragraphs in all of his letters about the contents and motivation of his ministry (Col. 1:24-29). He reminds them that he is a steward, with a divinely-given commission 'to make the word of God fully known' (Col. 1:25). His whole life has been a response to God's call to take the revelation of the mystery of God's otherwise secret plan to the Gentiles, the entire pagan world. As a steward, he has been entrusted with his Master's resources, which constitute the glorious treasure of the gospel, 'now revealed to his saints'. This then is the content of his ministry, 'which is Christ in you, the hope of glory' (1:27). Here is God's provision for the present – Christ Himself dwelling within His people. And flowing from that reality is the sure and certain hope for the future of coming glory. Verse 28 is both a glorious declaration, '<u>Him</u> we proclaim' (Christ, not just Christianity), and also an insight into the methodology of His preaching 'warning everyone and teaching everyone with all wisdom'.

But perhaps even more significant is the ultimate purpose of this stewardship of the gospel by the great apostle to the Gentiles. The proclamation, with its warning of the negatives and teaching the positives, is to this end – 'that we may present everyone mature in Christ'.

That apostolic purpose must surely govern all of us who stand in the true apostolic succession of the gospel, as we seek to fulfil the commission given directly by the Lord Jesus Himself to His apostles after His resurrection. 'Go ... and make disciples of all nations ... teaching them to observe all that I have commanded you' (Matt. 28:19-20). And this clearly specific command, to teach the nations, is one of those to be followed by disciples, in every generation and across the world. At one level it is a wonderfully uncomplicated goal, to 'present everyone mature in Christ', but it may easily degenerate into an overly simplistic definition of the teacher's task, unless we take the time to unpack what that 'maturity' consists of and how our teaching can promote and achieve this very demanding aim. But as we do that, we should remember that Colossians 1:29 is full of encouragement to embrace the challenge, through hard work and in dependence on the divine energy. Paul writes, 'For this I toil, struggling with all his energy that he powerfully works within me'. Without 'his energy' all our 'toil' would be in vain. But without our toil that energy will never be experienced in the church and the quest for maturity will be quickly abandoned.

For over fifty years now it has been my immense privilege and responsibility to seek to be a faithful preacher and teacher of the whole counsel of God, in the Scriptures. During that time I have learned a great deal about the dynamic power of the Word of God to transform lives through its careful exposition. I have seen people drawn to Christ through the spiritual magnetism of the Word preached, people at different ages and stages of life and from all sorts of different places and backgrounds. I have witnessed God's grace and truth building up churches, transforming and strengthening believers, developing godly character through many faithful labourers in many different countries. But I have also learned a great deal about myself and my fellow-preachers – how weak and ineffective we are, how easily diverted from God's priorities, how the other demand-levels of our everyday ministry can pressurize us into trading off the important in order to focus on what seems to us to be the urgent. During my life-time in ministry those pressures have only increased, exponentially, as they continue to do. Time for reflection and re-orientation is notoriously difficult to find, but I become more and more convinced that it is essential if our ministry is not just to survive, but to bear fruit that remains.

Towards the end of my time in local church pastoral ministry I discovered the great benefit of taking a day every two or three months, to be on my own with the Lord, dealing with the things I had shelved due to lack of time or energy, seeking to come to a sober assessment of the immediate past and the present situation, in the church, in my family, in myself and prayerfully thinking through future possibilities and direction. It often took me most of the morning just to unwind, to quieten my heart and to seek God's face. Later, when I worked in the training ministry of the Proclamation Trust through the Cornhill course, there was more opportunity for this sort of reflection to be built into my regular schedule, but I have never forgotten both the particular pressures of pastoral ministry and also its delights and fulfilments. That is what has generated my desire to attempt some encouragement for those who bear the heat and burden of the day and who may be growing weary in well-doing, in the regular ministry of teaching God's living and enduring Word.

My purpose in writing then is to call each of us who has any responsibility for teaching the Bible to others, to whatever groups and at whatever level, to stop and consider as we re-evaluate what we are doing and why we are doing it. Every generation faces its own particular challenges in ministry, as well as those which seem to have been constant throughout history. Ours is certainly no exception and so we need to identify some of the contemporary traps and pitfalls into which we can easily stumble, if we are not aware of our own blind spots. Perhaps more than anything else we need to re-discover, clarify and be convinced about the priorities which the Bible itself gives us, as we explore its examples of what the early church was taught and how it was applied to life.

As a stimulus towards doing this, I have been re-reading a book which first appeared sixty years ago, but which, as far as I am aware has never received the attention which I think it deserves. 'The Recovery of the Teaching Ministry' by Dr J. S. Glen, the sometime Principal of Knox College, Toronto, is an apologia for teaching to be at the very heart of Christian ministry. In the light of the past sixty years, its thesis is profoundly relevant still and even prophetic. Noting that the Gospel of John introduces the person of Christ as 'full of grace and truth' (1:14), Glen laments that in ministry the two are too often separated, which he sees exemplified in the division between the academy (theoretical) and the ministry (practical). As an ordination college principal, he observes that he deals with 'young scholars who are not at heart inclined to the ministry and young ministers who are not at heart inclined to scholarship'.[1] Scholarship is seen either on the one hand as an escape from the pressures and demands of ministry, or on the other as an obstacle to the 'real' work, to be overcome and left behind. We would be naïve to imagine that things are much different today. If anything, theological training has become increasingly academicised, as have the equivalents for most professions, with the outcome that degree results open doors to ministry.

Just recently, I asked an able and gifted young man currently in his theological training how his studies were going, to which he replied, 'Oh, really well! I have been told I could become a theological educator.' Somewhat mischievously I responded, 'You mean a pastor?' But he didn't.

Being a pastor-teacher (Eph. 4:11) is often regarded as being somewhat inferior academically, perhaps because the role of the teaching ministry has been so under-played, or even ignored in the churches. But for every academic theologian, we need a cohort of competent, educated pastor-teachers, because the future of the faith in the western world is, humanly speaking, dependent on them and their work. After a lifetime in Christian work, Dr Oliver Barclay, who was General Secretary of

1. 'The Recovery of the Teaching Ministry,' by J. S. Glen; Edinburgh, St. Andrew Press, 1960; p. 23.

the Universities and Colleges Christian Fellowship (UK), reflected on this situation in an article entitled, 'Where is Academic Theology Heading?', which was published in the December 2006 edition of the British monthly 'Evangelicals Now'. While in no way denigrating the need for good academic theological standards, he questioned whether the debates that interest the world of academic theology are, in fact, the ones that many people outside the universities care about. He concluded, 'Few university departments are able to help students to face the postmodern and relativistic fashions today, the secular challenges to Christianity, or the real ethical problems that confront the local churches'.

Since the article appeared, the conservative colleges have been moving to a much more practical training base, which is very heartening, but we must never lose sight of the guidance of the New Testament that training is designed to give the potential minister the knowledge and understanding to make him a 'man of God, competent, equipped for every good work' (2 Tim. 3:17). As Barclay comments, 'That, Paul says, is the true function of the Scriptures when they are rightly taught in the churches'.

These are not peripheral matters, but absolutely central to the health and well-being of the church and therefore to the continuance and spread of the gospel in every location and each generation. To quote Glen further, 'The teaching ministry insists that the substance of the Bible and of its faith, including the substance of the great confessions of the church, are essentially intelligible and must be communicated from one generation to another'. But he laments that, 'The evidence indicates, however, that the church is less concerned for this than for the noumenal and the subjective. Worship is exalted at the expense of preaching, the holy at the expense of the intelligible. Sermons are designed more for the feelings than for the mind ... their obvious subjectivity is at the same time a failure to provide instruction.'[2] If the pastors do not teach, the church has nothing to offer those who attend, beyond what they already know or think they have discovered. Church becomes boring and churches where people are bored will eventually become churches that are empty.

We need to acknowledge straightaway that there are no easy answers, no quick-fix solutions to these deeply ingrained problems and challenges. But that does not mean that we are at liberty to leave them unaddressed, in the hope that somehow the situation might improve. Rather, we need to rediscover the immense privilege and responsibility of the pastor-teacher week in and week out to preach God's Word and so to feed God's flock. It is the only investment of time of which the outcome will yield eternal dividends. It is, however, deeply counter-cultural, profoundly and consistently hard work, extremely humbling, and constantly demanding, and yet there is nothing so satisfying, energising and joyful as to be a fellow worker with God in His harvest field (1 Cor. 3:9).

Because all valid Christian ministry is derived from Christ and because such ministry is primarily a ministry of the Word, in the enabling of the Holy Spirit, the obvious place to begin is with the New Testament vocabulary which describes the calling. As Jesus told His disciples, 'It is the

---

2. J. S. Glen; ibid.; p. 26.

Spirit who gives life; the flesh is of no avail. The words that I have spoken to you are spirit and life' (John 6:63). So what are we doing when we seek to communicate God's word for the instruction, upbuilding, encouragement and consolation of His people (1 Cor. 14:3)? The main verbs used help us to answer this all important question.

Firstly, the task is to teach (*didasko*). In essence, the word means to convey information, knowledge or skills, so that the person accepting what is offered will develop their own abilities. Teaching offers and learning receives what is offered. So Paul can speak of the Ephesians 'learning' Christ (Eph. 4:20) through the teaching of the gospel. It is not surprising that the verb is used nearly forty times in the synoptic gospels to describe the ministry of Jesus. In the temple, in the synagogues, in the open air, to His disciples, to the crowds, to the religious leaders, Jesus is constantly teaching. Indeed, many times over in the gospel narratives He is addressed as 'Teacher' (*didaskolos*), or translated in the older English versions as 'Master'. The implications of this, the major ingredient of Christ's ministry, are significant, in that His teaching is effectively claiming to be revelatory of the purposes of God and of His kingdom, which gives His instruction a unique blend of information and authoritative command. He is able to reveal the mind and will of God, which is why 'they were astonished at his teaching, for he taught them as one who had authority and not as the scribes' (Mark 1:22). His teaching is therefore linked with His Christological claims. 'I do nothing on my own authority, but speak just as the Father taught me (*didasko*). And he who sent me is with me. He has not left me alone, for I always do the things that are pleasing to him' (John 8:28-29).

Because all authentic Christian ministry is Christ's ministry, through His apostles and proclaimers, it is not surprising that by the end of the New Testament period, in the pastoral epistles, this has coalesced into a body of propositional or doctrinal truth which it is the church's derived mission to be teaching. This is described as 'sound doctrine', or literally, 'healthful teaching' (see 1 Tim. 1:10; 2 Tim. 4:3; Titus 1:9, 2:1). It is also referred to as 'the teaching that accords with godliness' (1 Tim. 6:3), which is also the major thrust of the exhortation to Titus in the opening verse of the letter addressed to him. There is an urgency about these appeals since the health and well-being of the churches depend upon 'the pattern of sound words' (2 Tim. 1:13) being understood, preserved faithfully and then passed on, to build up believers in their faith and to contradict error (2 Tim. 2:2). The risen Lord's charge to His church to make disciples of all nations is to be accomplished by 'teaching them to observe all that I have commanded' (Matt. 28:20). That charge has never been rescinded and must be the heart of all ministry that seeks truly to honour Christ.

There are, however, other instructive words used, which help to deepen our understanding and broaden our perspectives regarding the teaching ministry. Of these, to proclaim or preach (kerysso) and to announce good news (angello) are the most frequently used. The nouns derived from these verbs have also become well known in the field of Biblical scholarship as 'Kerygma' is used to indicate both the act and content of proclamation, while the 'evangel' is usually taken to refer to the gospel (good news) which is being announced. In the former case (kerysso) the emphasis

lies in the authoritative nature of the proclamation, which
calls for compliant action. To ignore it is to reject it. In a
helpful and extensive article, examining the use of the verb,
L. Coenen states that '[kerysso] characterises the concrete
proclamation of the message in a particular instance, with
special reference to the claim that is being made, and its
authority to set up a new order. It includes information,
but is always more than mere instruction or a bare offer'.[3]
'Angello' and its derivatives, giving us our own terms such
as 'evangelizing', seem to have a more special focus, which
is described as 'the making known of God's activity, his
will to save.' Sometimes translated 'message', the emphasis
is on the veracity of what is stated or offered, because the
messenger represents, and therefore carries the authority
of, the sender. The Old Testament prophets fulfilled that
role as they spoke for the God of Israel, to proclaim His
mighty acts and His rescuing mercy. The New Testament
writers fulfil the same role with regard to the good news
of Jesus and we are to follow in their steps.

The content of this public ministry is expressed in a
wide variety of phrases, perhaps best summarised in Jude 3
as 'the faith that was once for all delivered to the saints' and
again in Jude 20 as 'your most holy faith'. For Paul, what he
proclaims is the 'gospel of God' (1 Thess. 2:8, 9), which is
Christ Himself (Col. 1:28), crucified (1 Cor. 1:23), raised
from the dead (1 Cor. 15:12), the Son of God, Jesus Christ
(2 Cor. 1:19). This is the 'message' to be fully proclaimed
so that all the Gentiles might hear it (2 Tim. 4:17). And

3. L. Coenen 'Proclamation,' in the 'New International Dictionary of
   New Testament Theology;' Vol. III, Paternoster Press, Exeter, 1978;
   pp. 46-56.

closely intertwined with the message of the gospel is the
need for its content to be unpacked and explained, in order
that those who have embraced its offer of salvation may
grow in their knowledge and love of their rescuer. The way
in is also the way on. Maturity is always the goal.

The message is fixed, non-negotiable, unchanging,
regarding both its content and its summons to repentance
and faith, but the verbs are many and scholars generally
agree that there is a great deal of interchangeability with
no one dominant, technical term. To the three verbs we
have mentioned can be added others, translated as saying,
confessing, witnessing, evangelising, making known,
delivering, prophesying. The great verse about preaching
(2 Tim. 4:2) provides us with something of the flavour
of the variety of ways in which Timothy was to fulfil his
charge. 'Preach the word … reprove, rebuke and exhort,
with complete patience and teaching.' Here preaching and
teaching are united in the same verse, which along with
other Biblical indications should warn us against making
more of the differences between them than the Biblical
usage would warrant. So much for the theory, but what
did it look like in practice?

The narrative of Philip and the Ethiopian eunuch in
Acts 8 provides a very valuable illustration of how this
combination of proclamation and teaching worked out in
the earliest days of the church. The event has often been
pressed into service as an evangelistic topic, or as a call to
involvement in mission, but it is perhaps undervalued in
terms of its instruction about how the Word of the Lord
was growing and multiplying. When Philip approaches the
chariot the scroll of Isaiah is open, but to the Ethiopian it

is a closed book. Philip's question opens the conversation, 'Do you understand what you are reading?' (v. 30). The narrative then revolves around three questions which the eunuch puts to Philip. 'How can I unless someone guides me?' (v. 31). 'About whom does the prophet say this?' (v. 34) 'What prevents me from being baptized?' (v. 37). These are the stages by which Philip's proclamatory-teaching ministry advances, on a one-to-one, personal level and they are surely recorded by Luke for our instruction.

Understanding is all important. The mind has first to be informed, illuminated and convinced, before the truth can operate within the heart to activate the will. But that understanding is dependent upon a human teacher. Could the Holy Spirit not open the eunuch's spiritual eyes from the page of Scripture without any human intervention? Of course He could, sometimes has, and sometimes may do so still. But the text here is very clear that the Spirit chose to use Philip ('Go over and join this chariot' v. 29) probably to indicate that his normal way of bringing light and life through the inspired Word is by means of a human teacher. If the pastor-teachers are not teaching the Scriptures by their interpretation and application the Bible will remain a locked book in the church and therefore an absent voice in the public forum. The sheep may gather for a time but they will not grow and they will not impact society outside of the fold.

The Ethiopian is looking for someone to guide him (v. 31). The verb means literally 'to lead the way'. This is the teacher's ministry – to listen to, comprehend and even anticipate the questions and issues raised by the text. Who is the one 'led like a sheep to the slaughter ... whose life is taken away from the earth?' (v. 32-33). Is it 'about himself or someone else?' (v. 34). So Philip, who has come to give understanding and to provide guidance, seizes the opportunity of the second question and 'beginning with this Scripture he told him the good news about Jesus' (v. 35).

How did Philip know how to interpret the Isaiah prophecy? Did the Holy Spirit grant him sudden super-natural illumination at that precise point? Perhaps, but it seems unlikely, since the whole Bible teaches us to use our minds rather than shelve them. It seems to me much more likely that Philip is presented to us here, by Luke, as a classic example of the teacher of others, who has first been taught himself. In his first volume, Luke has drawn our attention to this very section of Isaiah, the fourth song of the suffering servant of the Lord, in chapter 53. Significantly, in Luke 22:37 it is the Lord Jesus Himself who teaches His disciples about the fulfilment of the prophecy. Just before leaving the upper room for the garden of Gethsemane, His betrayal and arrest, Jesus says, 'I tell you that this Scripture must be fulfilled in me: "And he was numbered with the transgressors". For what is written about me has its fulfilment'. 'In me', 'about me'; Jesus has no doubt as to the meaning of Isaiah 53 and His fulfilment of the servant's substitutionary, atoning death. Nor does He want His disciples to be in any doubt.

After the cross and resurrection, the period until the ascension seems to have included special instruction for the disciples (see Acts 1:3) about His fulfilment of the Old Testament, so that they could interpret its message in the light of His saving work. Luke again stresses the point. 'Then [Jesus] said to them, "These are my words that

I spoke to you while I was still with you, that everything written about me in the Law of Moses and the Prophets and the Psalms must be fulfilled." Then he opened their minds to understand the Scriptures' (Luke 24:44-45). The teaching disciples were first taught by Jesus Himself.

Philip first appears in volume 2 of Luke's account in Acts 6:3-5 as one of the seven men 'of good repute and full of the Spirit and wisdom', appointed to serve the needs of the fast-growing Jerusalem church. Yet from Acts 2:42 we know that the believers 'devoted themselves to the apostles' teaching'. So Philip was clearly taught by the apostles, who were taught by Jesus, which enabled him to guide the eunuch into the truth of the gospel. But more than that, as he (literally) evangelised the Ethiopian, God granted his hearer understanding, repentance and faith in the Saviour, which meant that the final question, 'What prevents me from being baptised?' was answered by an inaudible, but resounding, 'Nothing'. The Ethiopian doubtlessly knew that this would be a costly decision. He had just come from Jerusalem, where Acts 8:1 tells us, 'there arose a great persecution against the church in Jerusalem and they were all scattered …' He was joining himself to what must have seemed a despised Jewish minority, rejected by the very orthodoxy which had presumably drawn him to Jerusalem to worship (v. 27). But he does so, aware of the fulfilment of all that the Old Testament prophesied, in the person and work of the suffering servant, the Son of God. Someone has guided him and given him understanding. He has received a teaching ministry. The eunuch's life has been transformed through his mind being informed of the good news through Philip's teaching.

However we are in a more privileged position than even Philip was. For us, with the completion of the sixty-six books of Scripture, we have not only the record of the divine self-revelation throughout salvation-history, but also the divinely inspired explanation and interpretation. This can be encapsulated in its most simple form by a verse such as 1 Corinthians 15:3, where we read both a fact and its interpretation, an event and its explanation, in the opening words, 'Christ died (fact) for our sins (explanation) according to the Scriptures (authority)'. Because the Bible is God's authoritative, infallible Word we know that its one divine author has provided us with both true truth and true interpretation, as we use the Scriptures to interpret Scripture, in all of the books and both of the testaments. So the message of the Christian teacher is gathered from the completed revelation, which is the content of all the Scriptures, yet always acknowledging that just as the text is God's gift, in the Word, so our understanding is also God's gift, through His Spirit. Surely the Lord is saying to us, through the Scriptures, what He said to Timothy, through Paul, 'Think over what I say, for the Lord will give you understanding in everything' (2 Tim. 2:7). This is the teacher's calling and the teacher's confidence.

If then we are called to lead and teach the path to salvation and spiritual maturity, we must be people of the Word of God both in our own personal lives and in every aspect of our ministry. Whether in pastoral counselling or chairing a business meeting, whether in bereavement-support or in planning corporate worship, we are to be ministers of the Word, every bit as much as when we stand to proclaim it publicly. But it is in our preaching that our true centre of confidence will be disclosed. Many preachers would say that they are Biblical, because they use the Bible in their talks – for ideas, inspiration, illustration, but primarily it is a tool in their hands. That is not Biblical exposition. I have tried to focus the problem in my teaching videos 'Equipped to Preach the Word' by using the analogy of a car and by asking the question, 'Where is the Bible in your "car"?', meaning your preaching ministry, or your church. For many evangelical preachers it is no longer in the boot or the back seat, but it is firmly anchored in the passenger seat, which means that it never gets its hands on the steering-wheel. That is the preacher's role. He drives the car. But in faithful expository preaching the Bible text drives the talk, in its contents, shape and application. The text is king, because when it is in the driving seat the voice of Christ is heard by all who have ears to hear. If Christ is truly to be the Lord of the church then His Word must be our rule and guide and He will mediate His authority through His Word, which endures for ever. Only preaching that relinquishes the driving seat to the text of God's Word will bring God-glorifying maturity to God's people.

Maturity must start in the preacher himself. Yielding to the lordship of Christ for the teacher means giving up any idea about ministry being about me and my fulfilment and identifying myself with John the Baptist's determination that Christ must increase and he decrease (John 3:30). If that was true of the great forerunner, of whom 'none born of women was greater' (Luke 7:28), how much more must it be so with us? I find it helpful to realise that when I think I can manipulate a Bible passage or select my own preferred ingredients from it, my behaviour is the opposite of humility. We can only be teaching others if we ourselves submit to being taught and that means the Word of the Lord in the driving seat. As Jesus Himself has instructed us, 'A disciple is not above his teacher, but everyone when he is fully trained will be like his teacher' (Luke 6:40). However long we have been serving we are all still in His training school and perhaps the longer our service, the more we realise that we are still actually in the kindergarten. There is no room for any sort of human pride or aggrandisement in the service of the King of kings. So, let us teachers of the Word humble ourselves under God's mighty hand and leave it to Him as to what doors He chooses to open and how He determines to use us. We could not do better, every time we speak, than to pray John Stott's life-long prayer, which it is said was framed above his bed.

> When telling Thy salvation free
> Let all absorbing thoughts of Thee
> My heart and soul engross.
> And when all hearts are bowed and stirred
> Beneath the influence of Thy Word
> Hide me behind Thy Cross.

The goal of preaching is spiritual maturity. That will require us, as preachers, constantly to strive not only to provide faithful Bible teaching to inform, but also to transform, both ourselves and our hearers. And that process can only be developed as the product of personal humility and deep dependence on God.

2.

Preaching that grows people

Every Biblical expository preacher will be challenged frequently by Paul's parting instruction to Timothy in 2 Timothy 4:2 to 'preach the word,' to keep examining our goals and practice, so as to ensure that we stay on the line of the truth, the whole truth and nothing but the truth. But we do not always connect that command with the explanations either side of it (2 Tim. 3:16-17 and 4:2b-4) as to why this is the indispensable heart of all ministry that pleases God and honours the Lord Jesus. In his paraphrase of Paul's letters, Prof F. F. Bruce presents Paul's teaching about the purpose of Scripture in these words. 'Every part of those writings is divinely inspired and useful for teaching truth and refuting error, for correcting the line of a man's life and instructing him in righteousness. By them the man of God may be completely fitted out, equipped for every good work.'[1] There again is that note of maturity, completeness, which we identified in Colossians 1:28, where the focus of Paul's ministry is 'to present everyone

---

1. 'An Expanded Paraphrase of the Epistles of Paul,' by F. F. Bruce; Paternoster Press Exeter, 1965; p. 321.

mature in Christ' (ESV), or 'perfect' (NIV), or 'fully grown' (Bruce).

What we are seeking to provide for our congregations each week must not be a subsistence diet, just enough to get them to survive another week, but a well-balanced and proportional nutrition plan, to enable them to grow and develop in every area of their discipleship. Its purpose is their maximum spiritual well-being. And that is not something we have to invent; it has already been provided by God in 'all Scripture'. So as I seek to preach the whole counsel of God, week by week, the Word will be doing its work, provided I am expounding it accurately, faithfully and according to its divine purpose (Isa. 55:11). There is a rich New Testament vocabulary, which should focus our exploration of what this apostolic purpose actually involved. We shall consider three of the major terms used, translated for us as growth, maturity and fullness.

The first, 'growth', puts the emphasis on the process by which the goal of maturity is to be reached. In Scripture, from the beginning (Gen. 2:9), God is the giver of life and the author of growth throughout His creation. 'You cause the grass to grow for the livestock and plants for man to cultivate' (Ps. 104:14). So it is not surprising that this often is used as a picture of the unseen spiritual development of His people which is God's priority. From the parable Jesus told of the sower and the soils (Mark 4:1-20), we learn that 'the sower sows the Word' (v. 14) and it is this seed which, when heard and accepted, 'bears fruit' (v. 20).

This concept continues and develops in apostolic thinking and practice, as, for example when Paul tells the Corinthians, 'I planted, Apollos watered, but God gave the growth. So neither he who plants nor he who waters is anything, but only God who gives the growth' (1 Cor. 3:6-7). Only God can give the spiritual growth and only as the Word is implanted in the believer. In context, Paul is rebuking the Christians at Corinth because they are not growing, they are still 'people of the flesh, infants in Christ', babies who are not yet weaned on to solid food (1 Cor. 3:1-2).

Growth, then, is not simply the sowing of the seed of the gospel and its reception in terms of repentance and faith, but the whole process of development from new birth and babyhood to adult maturity, from a seedling to the full fruit at harvest. This same thought, which describes the purposeful development of the individual believer, also applies of course to the church as an entity, whether universal or local. Church growth has become a major topic of concern during the past few decades, with a whole literature and culture emerging to teach its principles and practice, much of which can prove helpful. However, while we have constantly to remind ourselves that growth is totally dependent on God alone, this should lead us to pray, work and expect it to happen much more than we do. All the resources are already available in the gift of God's Word and the energising dynamic of the Spirit, so that the growth which God purposes is the natural fruit of the divine life planted within each individual believer. Indeed, it is only because the believer is 'in Christ' that any sort of spiritual growth can occur.

Growth, then, is the expected mode of the church's existence. As it grows, so it lives, which means that God's revealed truth and love in Christ are the energising life power of His body. This is Paul's aspiration for the Ephesian Christians when he encourages them, that, 'speaking the truth (literally "truthing") in love, we are to grow up in every way into him who is the head, into Christ, from whom the whole body joined and held together by every joint with which it is equipped, when each part is working properly, makes the body grow so that it builds itself up in love' (Eph. 4:15-16).

One of the greatest implications of this for our preaching is the reminder that growth is a gradual process, which is hardly observable on a day to day basis. We can tend the plants but we cannot make them grow. We can hoe the soil, remove the stones, deal with the weeds, but we do not produce the fruit. It has been rightly said that, when God ripens apples, He isn't in a hurry and He doesn't make a noise. So the preacher is in for a long haul, but confident that the seed has all the power needed to germinate and multiply. Like the farmer, in Jesus' parable, 'he sleeps and rises, night and day, and the seed sprouts and grows; he knows not how. The earth produces by itself, first the blade, then the ear, then the full grain in the ear' (Mark 4:27-28). But the harvest does come. The growth of the church, whether seen individually or corporately, is an ongoing process and will be until the day when 'we shall be like him, because we shall see him as he is' (1 John 3:2). However, we need to keep clear what the heart of that process is, what Biblical maturity will look like.

We shall need to explore this in more detail elsewhere, but suffice to say here that it is not conformity to the external standards or expectations of the evangelical sub-cultures to which we may belong. God's standard is conformity to Christ. 'For those whom he foreknew he also predestined to be conformed to the image of his Son' (Rom. 8:29). 'And we all, with unveiled face, beholding the glory of the Lord, are being transformed into the same image from one degree of glory to another. For this comes from the Lord who is the Spirit' (2 Cor. 3:18). Seven verses later, Paul reveals where we find 'the light of the knowledge of the glory of God'. It is 'in the face of Jesus Christ' (2 Cor. 4:6).

The second term directs us to what the purpose of growth is actually achieving and therefore what is its ultimate goal, and that is 'maturity'. The basic meaning, which has multiple connected references in the New Testament, is the consummation or conclusion of a dynamic process. Intention is fulfilled; the job is done. English synonyms talk about completion, the end or goal, adulthood, perfection. This latter term is not talking about moral perfection, meaning the absence of indwelling sin or behavioural flaws in the believer. Rather, it is the picture of the grown adult, who has now come of age, who demonstrates the integrated wholeness of their personality as a unique mature individual. Of course, this is an anticipation, in time, of the perfect wholeness which will only be ours in the eschatological kingdom of the new creation. So, in all the Bible's teaching about God's kingdom it is important to be clear about the distinction between what is ours already and what must await the life of the world to come.

This is so important because it will save us from a quest for what cannot be ours in a fallen, broken world – perfect healing, perfect freedom from sin, perfect love, the perfect church. I am reminded of the comment attributed to

Spurgeon that he had only once met a 'perfect' man and he
was a perfect nuisance! But so many become disillusioned
and stunted in their growth because they are trying by force
of their will, by massive efforts to stir up and increase their
'faith', to wrest from God's hands blessings which belong
to eternity. 'The Christian life in the New Testament is
not projected idealistically as a struggle for perfection, but
eschatologically as the wholeness which a person is given
and promised.'[2] Given in a measure now, but promised in
its fullness in eternity, this is not a mechanistic process,
but the glad involvement of heart and will to become in
practice what God declares us already to be 'in Christ', as
we grow up to maturity.

Frequently, the apostle Paul testifies to this central
experience of his own life, where the dynamic to live a
godly life is seen to be the divine gift, appropriated by
faith. 'I have been crucified with Christ. It is no longer
I who live, but Christ who lives in me. And the life I
now live in the flesh I live by faith in the Son of God,
who loved me and gave himself for me' (Gal. 2:20). Or
even more tellingly in Philippians 3:12, 'Not that I have
already obtained this (the resurrection from the dead) or
am already perfect, but I press on to make it my own,
because Christ Jesus has made me his own.' He concludes,
'One thing I do: forgetting what lies behind and straining
forward to what lies ahead, I press on toward the goal
for the prize of the upward call of God in Christ Jesus'
(vv. 13-14). For Paul, it is the future which dictates the

---

2. R. Schippers in 'The New International Dictionary of New Testament Theology,' Vol. 2, ed. Colin Brown; The Paternoster Press,
   Exeter, 1976; p. 65.

priorities of the present; the maturity, which will one day be his in the presence of his Lord, changed into his likeness, which dominates and energises his passion for growth in the here and now.

The third term revolves around the ideas of 'fulness', being filled, made complete, mission accomplished. The same term is used both of the process of being filled and the state of that having happened, which is fulness. As before, the origins of the New Testament's development of the theme go back to the very beginnings of the gospel; in this case as recorded by John. Perhaps we fail to give sufficient recognition to John 1:16, 'And from his (the Word made flesh) fulness we have all received, grace upon grace.' It is a verse with staggering implications, because verse 14 at the climax of John's prologue has just outlined for us what that actually means. In the Word becoming flesh and pitching His tent among us, 'we have seen his glory, glory as of the only Son from the Father, full of grace and truth.' The glory of God is not the focus of a spirituality of mystery. It is a clear, plain revelation in down-to-earth human terms which men and women can not only see, but share. With the coming of the Christ the way begins to open for sinful human beings to have a part in the glory of God, so that John can say that out of His fulness of grace and truth we have all received grace and truth (v. 17). But it takes the rest of the New Testament to unpack what that means.

The overflowing fulness motif appears again in John 7 with the great invitation of Jesus on the last day of the Feast of Tabernacles in the temple at Jerusalem. 'If anyone thirsts, let him come to me and drink.' Explaining that to drink means to believe in Him (literally 'into Him'),

Jesus promises that out of the believer's inner being will flow rivers of living water. John then exegetes this for us, his readers, by the statement, 'Now this he said about the Spirit, whom those who believed in him were to receive, for as yet the Spirit had not been given, because Jesus was not yet glorified' (vv. 37-39). The Spirit could only be given after Jesus had been lifted up on the cross. There could have been no Pentecost without Calvary. But in John's gospel the first words of the risen Lord, on Easter evening, to His disciples, confirmed both His commission to them and His enabling to fulfil it. 'As the Father has sent me, even so I am sending you. And when he had said this, he breathed on them and said to them, "Receive the Holy Spirit"' (John 20:21-22). No wonder then that the Pentecost account in Acts 2, tells us that 'they were all filled with the Holy Spirit' (v. 4) and began to tell in many tongues the mighty works of God (v. 11).

Because the gift of the spirit to every believer (see Acts 2:38-39 and Rom. 8:9-10) is described by the 'fulness' vocabulary, it is not surprising that the two concepts are closely interwoven throughout the apostolic writings. It is the ministry of the Holy Spirit, the Spirit of Jesus, to bring the fulness of Jesus into the heart, or innermost being, of each believer, so that the process of transformation, growing into the likeness of Christ, can become the norm of Christian experience. For example, the command in Ephesians 5:18 to 'be filled with the Spirit' is given only on the basis of the teaching earlier in the letter that God 'put all things under his (Christ's) feet and gave him as head over all things to the church, which is his body, the fulness of him who fills all in all' (1:22-23). The command is only possible in the light of the teaching. The indicatives necessarily prepare the way for the imperatives. Similarly, in Eph 3:19 Paul prays for his readers to be 'filled with all the fulness of God,' but earlier in the prayer we learn that can only happen as God's people are 'strengthened with power by his Spirit in your inner being, so that Christ may dwell in your hearts through faith' (vv. 16-17). The fulness is found only in Jesus, but the experiential awareness of that reality in the believer's heart and life is the fruit of the Holy Spirit's indwelling.

Colossians is a somewhat parallel letter, but the teaching here is even more specific. The great Christological passage in 1:15-18 concludes with the affirmation that 'in him (Christ) all the fulness of God was pleased to dwell' (v. 19). Paul's point is that there could not possibly be any greater 'fulness' than God Himself and there could therefore be no alternative source of that fulness than Christ, the Word made flesh. To seek to add anything to the fulness of God's glory in Christ is actually to subtract from His uniqueness, majesty and splendour. Perhaps the key sentence in the whole letter is 2:9-10. 'For in him (Christ) the whole fulness of deity dwells bodily and you have been filled in him, who is the head of all rule and authority.' Or, as Bruce paraphrases it, 'It is in Christ that you have found your completion – in Christ, who is the Head of every principality and power'.[3] The verses which follow reveal that it is through the cross and resurrection that Christ has gained this victory, which enables us to participate in His triumph. Whatever the alternatives on

3. Bruce; op. cit.; p. 253.

offer to supply fulness of life, meaning and fulfilment, in Colossae, whether the empty deceit of philosophy and human traditions (2:8), mystical experiences (2:18), or self-made religion in asceticism and severity to the body (2:23), they are all an empty sham, of no value, a waste of time and energy compared with the fulness of and in Christ, 'who is your life' (3:4).

Understanding these concepts and the central position they occupy in the New Testament's teaching about the Christian life is essential if our contemporary ministries are in any significant way to reflect the divinely-given apostolic priorities and practice. But such understanding is also wonderfully enriching and motivating. To know that God is committed to the growth of His people, both in quantity and quality, is a powerful stimulus to our own evangelism and teaching. Every time we open God's Word and seek to preach it to others, faithfully and accurately, we are handling a treasure whose power to transform lives is limitless. We never can predict what God will do, even through our preaching, and, for our good, we probably never will know. However, we shall want to be unashamed workmen, as we give ourselves to the task of rightly handling God's Word of truth. We should surely keep asking ourselves whether this piece of teaching I am currently preparing will be enabling growth. Where is its nutrition for the soul? What are the practical steps that need to be spelt out and taken, for its transformational purpose to be fulfilled, so that knowledge becomes life-style?

Am I giving my hearers a greater vision of the maturity which can be theirs in Christ? What is there in the passage to encourage us all to hunger and thirst for God, His kingdom and His righteousness? Am I presenting that truth as positively and motivationally as God enables me to do, by working it first into my own life and soul? Let us keep asking God to give us a clearer understanding of the fulness that is found in Christ alone and to use that truth to discern and reject the multitude of fake claims that are paraded before us by our culture, day after day. Above all, let us drink deeply of Jesus, to experience the inflow and overflow of His Spirit within our inner beings, to become rivers of life-giving water, in the church and in the world. These are the values that matter most, from which everything else can flow, which is why they were the apostles' great concern and the heart-beat of their teaching ministry.

However, before we leave this important theme, we must try to sharpen the lens a little, to identify what is the heart-beat of our Christian life and growth. It is very easy to regard growth to maturity and fulness as a somewhat mechanical process, which can come to be thought of as something external, something that happens to us, provided the right ingredients are being employed; but in a rather impersonal way. It would be a bit like a chemical experiment – mix the ingredients together and the reaction will occur. Go through the right training course, learn the essential doctrines, be around keen Christians and the rest will follow. But that sort of mechanistic approach to developing Christian maturity, although it includes valuable and necessary ingredients, is prone to ignore the one element of Christian living which actually matters most, which is our individual and personal relationship with God. From that foundation everything else is built.

The primacy of love could not be more clearly stated than by the Lord Jesus Himself in the gospels (see Matt. 22:40, Mark 12:30, Luke 10:27). In its fullest form, in Mark, Jesus' response to the question about the most important commandment begins by quoting the words of the Shema from Deuteronomy 6:4-5. Because, the Lord is one, 'You shall love the Lord your God with all your heart and with all your soul and with all your mind and with all your strength'. The original text in Deuteronomy does not include the mind, and what is often translated 'strength' in English is literally 'muchness' in Hebrew. It is not so much a reference to physical energy as to totality, loving God 'to total excess', in Christopher Wright's words. It is suggested that Jesus added the 'mind' because by the first century the term 'heart' had narrowed somewhat from its earlier meaning. If we reckon that the original wording indicated a response of the whole being (heart and soul) we shall not be misled. The heart, in Biblical thinking, is not the seat of the emotions, but the control-centre of the personality where decisions are made which determine the course of life. When Jesus adds the 'mind' He is perhaps focusing on the understanding and the impact which that will inevitably have on one's actions. The 'soul' is the term more usually employed to indicate the inner self, the emotions and desires. All of these constituent ingredients of the complex phenomenon we call human personality are to be dedicated to loving God 'to total excess'.

This is the ideal set before us, throughout the Bible, and it must therefore be the key single factor in our growing to maturity as Christian believers. Later, in Deuteronomy 10:12-13, this love for God is spelt out in practical detail. 'And now, Israel, what does the LORD your God require of you, but to fear the LORD your God, to walk in all His ways, to love him, to serve the LORD your God with all your heart and soul, and to keep the commandments and statutes of the LORD, which I am commanding you today for your good?' Here the central concept of love is saved from being reduced to a warm emotional response and given the solid content of reverent awe, godly conduct, unlimited service and careful obedience. This is what it means to love the Lord with all one's 'muchness'. In the Old Testament context this love is the expression of Israel's acceptance of the covenant relationship into which God has brought them, as His people, through the Passover deliverance and the revelation of Himself in the giving of the law. The covenant grace of God in salvation and deliverance from Egypt was designed to generate the response of love and obedience, in loyalty to their covenant Lord, which was the distinguishing mark of their relationship with Him. The same note is often repeated in Deuteronomy, of which 11:1 is a representative example. 'You shall therefore love the LORD your God and keep his charge, his statutes, his rules and his commandments always.' Love and obedience are inseparably linked (see also 11:13, 11:22, 13:3-4, 19:9). This explains why the Lord Jesus told His disciples, 'If you love me, you <u>will</u> keep my commandments' (John 14:15).

Love for God is no optional extra to be indulged when we feel like it; it is the heart and soul of the response of saved sinners to the grace of God in His covenant mercy.

But that is precisely the point that must always be made
as we encourage one another to grow in our love for the
Lord. As John put it so succinctly, 'In this is love, not that
we have loved God but that he loved us and sent his Son
to be the propitiation for our sins' (1 John 4:10). And
again, 'We love because he first loved us' (1 John 4:19).
For the Christian our love for God is an expression of our
gratitude for covenant grace, expressed in covenant loyalty
and issuing in obedience. It is the personal experience of
this amazing grace that is the experiential assurance and
conviction at the heart of our personal relationship. In
Peter Craigie's words, 'God's love and choice of his people
could not be known clearly in a philosophical or theological
sense; it was known rather through the experience of God
maintaining his covenant and loving kindness with his
faithful people ... known by two characteristics: they were
those that love him and those that keep his commandments'
(comment on Deut. 7:7-9).[4] Above all, this response of love
is relational, but it is only possible because of the prior
intervention of God in His grace.

This comes out most clearly in the later chapters of
Deuteronomy where perhaps the dominant issue is how
sinful Israel will ever be able to make this response of
continuing covenant love consistently. It's a familiar
challenge to us all, even under the new covenant, since
the nearer we come to God the more conscious we are
of how far short we fall. In William Cowper's hymn
'Hark, my soul' he expresses what we must all confess in
his concluding stanza, which begins, 'Lord, it is my chief

---

4. 'The Book of Deuteronomy,' by Peter C. Craigie; Eerdmans, Grand
   Rapids, 1976; p. 180.

complaint that my love is weak and faint'. So what is the remedy? Deut. 30:6 provides the answer. 'And the LORD your God will circumcise your heart ... so that you will love the LORD your God with all your heart and with all your soul, that you may live'. Christopher Wright's pithy summary captures this essential truth for us. 'The fundamental demand of the law (to love God with all one's heart and soul) is presented as the ultimate fruit of God's grace in the human heart.'[5]

For the new covenant believer this has been fulfilled 'by the circumcision of Christ', which Paul describes as 'a circumcision made without hands, by putting off the body of the flesh' (Col. 2:11). It is through the love of God, revealed in Christ, that the dynamic for change becomes possible, as the gift of the Spirit in consequence of His victory at Calvary and in His glorious resurrection produces His distinctive fruit, which is love (Gal. 5:22). Just as Israel did not receive God's love and grace due to any merits of her own, but it was because the Lord loved her that He loved her (Deut. 7:7-8), so the assurance for the new covenant believer is that 'nothing will be able to separate us from the love of God in Christ Jesus our Lord' (Rom. 8:39).

Too often Christians in our generation have become hesitant about expressing our love for Christ. This is partly a reaction against contemporary 'worship' songs, which utilise the metaphors and musical clichés of secular love songs, as though our expression of love for God were simply a more 'spiritual' version of that genre. It is also

---

5. 'Deuteronomy' in the New International Bible Commentary by Christopher J. H. Wright; Hendrickson Publishing, Peabody MA, U.S.A., 1996; pp. 289-290.

a right emphasis on the obedience of the life, shown in practical righteousness, as the indicator of true worship, rather than an emotional 'high' or a warm fuzzy feeling. But avoiding either extreme, we do need to encourage one another in our churches to grow in our love for the Lord. Yet this will come about not by concentrating on our love, our feelings, even our obedient service, but on the Lord God Himself and developing a Biblically healthy obsession with Him. Just as the Bible is God's book about Himself before it is God's book about us, so the gospel and growth in the Christian life is about God's love for us supremely in the cross of Jesus, before it is about our imperfect response. For the pastor-teacher, this means that teaching all that God reveals of Himself in any passage of Scripture is of far greater importance and lasting effectiveness in stimulating our love for God than trying to cultivate a humanly engendered response.

Fifty years ago, Francis Schaeffer wrote a book, which has not perhaps become as well-known as it deserves to be, on the theme of what Biblical spirituality is and how it can be developed. 'The Christian system of thought and life begins', he writes, 'with a God who is infinite and personal, with a strong emphasis on his personality.' The key to understanding how that relationship can work and grow lies in recognising the combination of God's infinity (which is why He can deal with each of us personally) and His own person-hood (which is why He can relate to us in the depths of our beings, since He has made us in His image). He goes on to point out that God deals with us firstly on the basis of what He Himself is and secondly on the basis of what He has made us. It is always a <u>personal</u> relationship, never merely mechanical or formal, but a genuine meeting of hearts and minds in self-giving love. 'So the command is to love God with all our heart, soul and mind. He is satisfied with nothing less than my loving him. I am not called merely to be justified. Man was created to be in personal fellowship with God and to love him.'[6] When we understand and preach that, as the dynamic for our Christian growth to maturity, it will bring vitality, refreshment, growth and fulfilment to us and to our hearers as nothing else can or will. And by God's grace it will bring glory to Him!

---

6. 'True Spirituality,' by Francis A. Schaeffer; Tyndale House Publishers, Wheaton IL U.S.A., 1971; pp. 148-149.

3.

Preaching in line with God's agenda

Throughout church history, every generation of preachers has had to face the challenge of proclaiming the unchanging message of the Scriptures to the particular context of their own time and culture. While the content of the Bible's teaching always remains constant, the preacher's task is to communicate that truth, the whole truth and nothing but the truth, to his own distinctively different cultural environment. He has to build a bridge between the historical context of whichever part of Scripture he is expounding and the (to him) modern world, in which he and his hearers live and work. He needs to be a preacher who connects. In J. I. Packer's memorable phrase he must be someone who 'mediates a meeting with God' for his listeners.

But why does it need a preacher to do that? If you can read a newspaper surely you can read the Bible for yourself. Of course, but reading is only the beginning of the process. Whenever we read, we also interpret what we are reading, whether the newspaper or the Bible. In the case of the Bible, even the process of translation involves a degree of interpretation and the multiple contemporary translations in English are witness to the concern and zeal of the translators to connect as accurately as possible to the culture they are serving. In the Preface to the original edition of the New International Version, perhaps the most widely used English translation, the translators affirm that their first concern was 'the accuracy of the translation and its fidelity to the thought of the biblical writers'. They continue, 'Because thought patterns and syntax differ from language to language, faithful communication of the meaning of the writers of the Bible demands frequent modifications in sentence structure and constant regard for the contextual meaning of words.'[1]

The translator, but also the preacher, is grappling with the fact that the living and enduring Word of God in Scripture is given in the words of human beings in a particular language and at a particular point in history. Just as the incarnation of our Lord Jesus Christ is a mystery in terms of the perfect blending of the human and the divine, so Scripture blends the historical human particularity of the text with its divinely inspired, eternal significance and validity. God spoke to real people in real situations, which is why the preacher has to become a diligent student of the text, if he is to be faithful to its original purpose. If we don't work hard rightly to understand what the text meant to its first readers or hearers, we shall certainly not be able to relay its message with any degree of clarity or authority to our contemporary context.

Whenever we approach a text, we are inevitably wearing our invisible set of prescription lenses. Our 'insight' is

1. Preface to NIV Study Bible, 1985; Zondervan, Grand Rapids; p. xi.

conditioned by our own prior understanding of the content it conveys, which in turn is heavily influenced by our own unique set of personal experiences that build up the texture of our lives. Yet this is never merely individual, since our thinking is responsive at every level to the pressures of the culture around us, whether our reactions to it are positive or negative. We are the product, at least in part, of the age and place we inhabit, although for the most part we are unaware of this, because our lenses have defined 'normality' for each of us.

As we enter the third decade of the twenty-first century, with its exponential rate of social change, fuelled by unbelievably fast and far-reaching technological developments, we preachers may well feel that we face a bewildering variety of challenges. On the one hand, at least in the west, the cultural norms have shifted almost beyond recognition, in my own life-time. Contemporary popular secular culture is omnipresent, raucous and assertive, demanding that its code of liberal laissez-faire be heeded, accepted and obeyed. Rooted in post-modernism, the self becomes the ultimate authority and central point of reference for most in today's culture. In this me-centred world, where my own experience and judgment are the ultimate arbiters, relativism quickly morphs into personal absolutism. So what I think <u>must</u> be true, because I think it. What I want <u>must</u> be good, because I'm worth it. What contradicts me <u>must</u> be resisted and eliminated, because the world revolves around me.

Now, of course, in one sense there is nothing new under the sun. Ever since the fall human beings have been intent on carving out our independence from God, to live my life as I choose without any reference to the Creator, who gives me every breath I breathe. In the famous words of W. E. Henley, 'I thank whatever gods there be for my unconquerable soul'.[2] But the technological revolution puts an entirely different complexion on the challenge of cultural connection, not least because it is increasingly difficult to secure attention to any message for long enough to be able to explore its contents in any depth. In an age of instant messaging, sound bites and strap lines, where the impression made seems to matter more than the content communicated, it is not easy to distinguish truth (if you even believe such a thing could exist) from falsehood – hence the phenomenon of 'fake news'. By contrast, when the Book of Common Prayer was published in 1662, one of the Advent prayers could ask, regarding the Holy Scriptures, 'that we may in such wise hear them, read, mark, learn and inwardly digest them, that by patience and comfort of thy holy word, we may embrace, and ever hold fast the blessed hope of everlasting life.' Today we might hear and perhaps read, but to mark, learn and inwardly digest are increasingly foreign concepts in a world dedicated to immediate information and instant responses. Analysis, evaluation and critical appraisal belong to a fast disappearing age. They seem irrelevant in a culture where assertion rather than argument prevails and where the loudest voices are the most likely to be heeded.

We are all familiar enough with this picture, not least because we all experience these cultural pressures ourselves as we seek to cope with the innumerable demands of

2. William Ernest Henley, poet (1849–1903) – 'Invictus'.

our own frenetic, busy lives. It is important that we are informed about and made aware of such powerful currents, but it is surely more important that we should know how to respond to them, how to navigate the choppy waters they are producing. Historically, the church has sometimes assimilated its faith and life to the dominant pressures exerted by the culture in which it lives. At other times it has generated so much opposition to the predominant cultural values that it has effectively retreated into a ghetto fortress-mentality, pulled up the drawbridge and allowed its vitality to be channelled almost exclusively into what is going on inside the castle walls. And today we can see the same responses modelled in many church pulpits.

On the one hand, the cultural values of choice, comfort, pleasure and fulfilment dictate the nature and content of much contemporary preaching. It becomes therapeutic, reassuring and ultimately undemanding. The emphasis is always on God's love, but rarely on His holiness. The Biblical call to repentance is reduced to 'saying sorry to God for our sins'. Faith is redefined as believing strongly enough that He will give me whatever I want from Him, because His greatest desire is to see me fulfilled since I'm special. And when that doesn't happen then I need to try harder, to work up more faith. Yet on the other hand, there can develop such a world-negating view of our culture that we retreat into a 'spiritual' bubble, which then assesses and approves its own 'effectiveness' on the basis of a withdrawn, detached, credal intellectualism. This becomes knowledge without love, truth without relationships, orthodoxy without warmth. It builds impregnable defences around the city, but rarely ventures out beyond its walls. With everything neat and tidied up, it has little interest in, and less to say to, the mess of human life that exists outside.

What both approaches have in common is that we are firmly in control, in the driving seat of what is preached and modelled in the churches and we soon begin to dig in to our own favoured positions, in order to defend and sustain them. Before long the Bible's priorities start to become subordinated to our goals and programmes and imperceptibly we start to drift into a spiritual culture which is actually being driven by the secular world around us, whether we embrace it or reject it. In an article entitled 'When "the good place" goes bad', Brian Colmery points out the pick and choose bespoke spirituality, what he calls the 'choose your own adventure' spirituality, in much western church culture. He writes, 'There is a conspicuous absence of anything ever making demands on us we wouldn't choose for ourselves. In Tim Keller's words, the universe never "crosses our will". It never decides we shouldn't do something we would like to do, or that we should do anything we'd prefer to avoid. We have a way of getting spiritual <u>and</u> staying in control.'[3]

So, how can we avoid being conformed to this world, or age, as Paul puts it (Rom. 12:2)? As we saw in chapter 1, whether it is in the area of our personal lives or our public ministry, the answer has to be a change of control in the driver's seat. I have to get out of that seat, along with all my preconceived contemporary values and ideas, and allow the Word of God to be in control. That is how God mediates

3. 'When "the good place" goes bad,' by Brian Colmery, posted by The Gospel Coalition website; 14.02.20.

His authority within the church and how the Holy Spirit energises and equips the body of Christ for its ministry in the world (Eph. 4:12ff). Through the ministry of God's Word sinners are saved, Christians are matured, churches are built and communities are transformed. It has always been this way and it will always be the divine methodology. The Spirit of God takes the Word of God to do the work of God. And there is no Plan B!

What we need to do now is to discover or re-examine the priorities of Scripture with regard to teaching our congregations, so that in terms of content, as well as emphasis and method, we become increasingly Biblical in our teaching and practice. What ought we to be aiming for and what are the Bible's instructions about how to reach these goals? That is the adventure of faith which we need to embrace and to which I hope this book may make a small, but positive, contribution.

There can be no doubt that we stand at a critical point for the future of orthodox Christian belief and practice in the western world. There has been a great deal of helpful analysis of our current predicament over the past thirty years, which cannot be reproduced here, but it should be read and digested by all of us contemporary preachers if we want to understand the multiple complexities of the presuppositions which we and our congregations all too often assume. Failure to do this may mean that what we say remains faithful, but largely unheard, because we fail to connect to where people are. To pretend that does not matter is to fly in the face of the way Jesus taught, the apostles preached and the prophets challenged, where time after time the eternal truth of the message is explicitly tailored to the specific context of the hearers. The Pentecost sermon in Acts 2 is very different from the Areopagus address in Acts 17, though the same gospel is of course preached. Both these proclamations are geared to the very different contexts of those being addressed. We should thank God that we are not without wise and penetrating counsellors in this matter.

Beginning with his title 'God in the Wasteland' in 1994, Professor David F. Wells has produced a wide-ranging series of critiques of western evangelicalism, culminating in 'The Courage to be Protestant' (2008).[4] They are Christ-centred, warm-hearted, Biblically focussed but devastating exposures of how far evangelical churches have moved from their historical confessional foundations in an ultimately depressing and unsuccessful attempt to adjust to the postmodern world. They should be read and re-read by all of us who preach.

More recently Os Guinness has produced an out-standing contribution to our understanding with his title 'Renaissance – the power of the gospel however dark the times'. He writes, 'At the heart of the crisis of the church in the advanced modern world, we need to recognize how modernity has had the effect of shifting the church from an integrated faith to a fragmented faith, from a stance under authority to a stance of preferences, and from a supernatural sense of reality to a purely secular perspective.'[5] While recognising the great work that has been done to develop a healthy rejection and critical riposte

---

4. 'God in the Wasteland,' by David F. Wells, 1994; IVP Leicester and 'The Courage to be Protestant,' 2008; IVP, Nottingham.

5. 'Renaissance,' by Os Guinness, 2014; IVP U.S.A.; pp. 37-38.

to the obvious challenges and attacks of the new atheism and relativism, he goes on to warn that 'we generally pay less attention to subtler trends that are also dangerous – such as the fashionable modern obsession with public opinion, numbers, quantity and metrics.'

The passage that follows illustrates just how much the western churches have bought in to the prevailing cultural assumptions, usually unconsciously, which ultimately leads to Christianity becoming merely a religious veneer applied to a thorough-going secularism. However, the whole thesis is an exposition of Christian hope, whatever the current climate. 'As always, faithfulness is all, and the circumstances are beside the point ... Let it be clearly understood that our hope in the possibility of renewal is squarely grounded, not in ourselves, not in history and the fact that it has happened before, but in the power of God demonstrated by the truth of the resurrection of Jesus.'[6]

One further piece of recommended reading, which is an insightful cultural and historical survey of evangelicalism in the western world since the Reformation is a paper by Ranald Macaulay entitled 'Being (even more) human'.[7] Dealing with a catalogue of misleading models of what the normal Christian life should look like, which he traces to their roots in the pietism of the early eighteenth century, Macaulay identifies a reductionist Christianity which effectually obscured or even denied what Francis Schaeffer called 'the lordship of Christ over the whole of life'. Whether intentionally or not, this led to the view

6. ibid., p. 144.

7. In 'Firstfruits of a New Creation' – essays honouring Jerram Barr; White Blackbird Books, U.S.A., 2019; p. 7.

that evangelism was the only valid purpose of life, 'often
accompanied by anti-intellectualism, that said, "The
Bible doesn't need human reasoning, it just needs to be
proclaimed. Getting to grip with the ideas of the culture
is a waste of time". The development of a Christian mind
was taboo even at university. The result was that few
Christians had the faintest idea how to challenge the
scepticism surrounding them.' We have suffered from
this reductionist view for a very long time, and it has
contributed to our general weakness both in presenting the
gospel powerfully to our culture and in developing Biblical
thinking, a Christian mind, within us as preachers and our
church congregations. The answer, however, is not cultural.
It is in the Word of God, in Biblical truth being fearlessly
and faithfully preached and practised.

One of the most acute observers and wisest of contemporary leaders within evangelicalism has summed up the
challenge in these terms. 'Much of what we have seen in our
secular moment is a battle between revolution and revelation.
The secular worldview eventually displaced a biblical
worldview. Eventually, all claims of divine revelation became
meaningless in a secular space. In the academy, there is an
ever increasing hostility to any claim of revelation ... The
church is the final place in a hyper-modern society where
the statement 'God says' makes any sense at all – but it had
better make total sense in the church.'[8]

What all of these wide-ranging and insightful treatments of the current malaise have in common is that they
see the answer in terms of a renewed confidence in the

8. 'The Gathering Storm,' by J. Albert Mohler Jr.; Nelson Books, Nash-
ville, U.S.A., 2020; pp. 194-195.

inspiration, truthfulness and sufficiency of Scripture and its consequent undiluted and unapologetic proclamation and exposition. The answer lies in the first instance with the preachers and teachers, with all the Bible-handlers from the kindergarten to the retirement home. However, this is the special responsibility of those who are set apart to the ministry of prayer and the Word as the pastor-teachers in the multitude of local churches across the world. Albert Mohler comments further, 'The other great truth to keep in mind is that God is always faithful to his Word. The church is not at risk of being embarrassed before the world for holding on to God's Word ... If we take our stand upon the revelation of God, no revolution— not even a revolution of sex and gender—can confuse us. If we take our stand in any other authority, every revolution will engulf us.'

Humanly speaking, the future of the church in western culture lies in the hands of the pastor-teachers. It has always been so. When the pulpits have been Biblically faithful, empowered by the Holy Spirit and engaged with the realities of the hearers' lives the churches have been vibrant, effective and growing. Sadly, the opposite has also been true. So, when the church seems weak and sickly, or sunk in a comfortable sleep of indifference, both the responsibility and the remedy lie with the pastor-teachers to proclaim the whole counsel of God, in prayerful dependence on the work of the Spirit, both in their preparation and their proclamation. This is the office to which God has delegated responsibility, as His agents, for the health and vitality of His flock (Eph. 4:11-16). 'This is how one should regard us, as servants of Christ and stewards of the mysteries of God. Moreover, it is required of stewards that they be found trustworthy' (1 Cor. 4:1-2).

Faithfulness is far more important than worldly measurements of success, which is why we need to have clear aims and objectives in view, as revealed to us in the Scriptures, so that we can seek to fulfil the purposes God has for us in our ministry. That is what matters most. The purposes belong to God and not to us. The enabling comes from God and not merely our human abilities. But the temptation is to think about what we do as <u>our</u> work for God, rather than <u>God's</u> work through us. We continually need the reminder of Paul's corrective to the Corinthians. 'What then is Apollos? What is Paul? Servants through whom you believed, as the Lord assigned to each. I planted, Apollos watered but God gave the growth. So neither he who plants nor he who waters is anything, but only God who gives the growth' (1 Cor. 3:5-7).

But in an age obsessed with celebrity, where the number of followers and 'likes' is the measure of value and where comparative statistics continually pitch one church against another, it is all too easy to succumb to the fatal temptation to think that it is all about me and my ministry. Isn't that at the heart of the blitz of temptations Jesus faced at the very beginning of His public ministry? To put His own needs first (stones into bread), to be given authority and glory (without the cross), to produce spectacular evidence of His deity (and amaze the crowds), each presented a subtle and attractive diversion from what He knew to be His Father's will (see Luke 4:1-13). Should we think that we shall be immune from similar temptations? So what are we allowing our hearts to believe about the purpose and priorities of our own ministry? So many ministers are deluded by their own constructed idols of what 'success' should look like, which will always lead to disappointment and despondence, because the true focus and purpose have been subtly distorted. If 'the chief end of man is to glorify God and enjoy him forever,' then ministry will be no exception. Whose glory am I really seeking?

As always, our Lord Jesus Christ is the perfect model for us. Just as He defeated the devil in the wilderness by prioritising the will of God as revealed in His Word, so in His ministry He exemplified and taught what the true service of God looks like. His dialogues with the Jews, in John chapters 5–8, are particularly rich with insights into His own submission, as man, to the Father's will and plan. 'Truly, truly, I say to you the Son can do nothing of his own accord, but only what he sees the Father doing. For whatever the Father does, that the Son does likewise' (John 5:19). And later, 'My teaching is not mine, but his who sent me' (John 7:16). But neither is He slow to point out the distortion that occurs when the wrong 'glory' motivates the heart. 'How can you believe, when you receive glory from one another and do not seek the glory that comes from the only God?' (John 5:44). And even more tellingly, 'The one who speaks on his own authority seeks his own glory, but the one who seeks the glory of him who sent him is true, and in him there is no falsehood' (John 7:18).

So whose glory am I really seeking? If all my speaking and teaching is submitted to the authority of God's Word alone, as I seek to proclaim its truth, the whole truth and nothing but the truth, then all the glory must belong to God, for everything in its content and proclamation are His gift, activated by His Spirit. But if, subtly, it has degenerated into being about my glory, pursuing my cultural idols of numbers, success, human approval and acclaim, that must be because my ultimate authority has become my own judgment and so my own glory has become my greater concern.

We need to repent collectively of the idolatry of quantitative measurements in ministry. It was Satan's incitement of David to number Israel that caused God's displeasure and judgment on the king and his people and led David to confess 'I have sinned greatly ... I have acted foolishly' (1 Chron. 21:1-8). Although this is a strange incident in many ways, it seems clear that David's own glory was his motivation, rather than giving glory to the God who had prospered his reign and extended the nation. The danger is that pursuing numerical growth can lead to a pragmatism, which argues that if something 'works' it must be good, it must have God's blessing. This is perhaps one of the more injurious downloads we have received from the church growth movement. As George W. Peters points out in his balanced Biblical critique, quantitative measures are deceptive because positive responses can be induced mechanically or psychologically, resulting in what he describes as 'an increase of a body without the development of muscle or vital organs'.[9]

Of course we all want the gospel to spread, but not by the dilution of its unchanging truth. That would not be gospel growth at all. Such thinking will inevitably lead us on a collision course with Scripture, which recognises over and over again that the gospel will not usually generate a positive response. It remains 'a stumbling block to Jews

---

9. See 'A Theology of Church Growth,' by George W. Peters; Zondervan, Grand Rapids, U.S.A., 1981.

and folly to Gentiles' (1 Cor. 1:23), because 'the god of this
world has blinded the minds of the unbelievers, to keep
them from seeing the light of the gospel of the glory of
Christ, who is the image of God' (2 Cor. 4:4). And he is still
actively about his work of intensifying that blindness, as
Jesus warned us, because 'false Christs and false prophets
will arise and perform great signs and wonders, so as to
lead astray, if possible, even the elect' (Matt. 24:24).

It is one of his clearest strategies to dupe the church
into replacing gospel truth as the agent of growth, with
contemporary methodology serving the agenda of pragmatism. If teaching the truth can be caricatured as
academic, cerebral and impractical, then the way is open
either to reduce or even to evacuate Biblical content from
our agenda. Further, if aspects of the truth are deemed to
be offensive to the modern mind, then they will be ignored,
or only occasionally mentioned, so as not to disturb the
comfort of those who have come to regard the church as
their spiritual health spa. Further still, if it is decided that
the modern mind is incapable of prolonged concentration,
or dealing with any content more demanding than a series
of sound bites, truth will be replaced by trivia and edification by entertainment. Pragmatism triumphs and the
objective revelation of God in His living and enduring
Word of Scripture is no longer in the driving seat, but
relegated back to the car boot.

An inevitable consequence, of course, is a lack of serious-
ness about Biblical ministry, which means less hard work
in the Scriptures by way of preparation for the preacher,
less satisfying content in what is said for the hearers and a
general reduction of the level of church experience to that

of the primary school. That may be great for children of primary school age, but not for adults, whose capacity for intelligent thought is far greater than many preachers seem to recognise. 'Why do our preachers simply patronise us and talk down to us?' is a question I have been asked several times by a variety of different church goers over the years. As John McArthur has said, if we preachers will concern ourselves with the depth of what we teach, God will see to its breadth. And as Paul exhorted the Corinthians, 'Brothers, do not be children in your thinking. Be infants in evil, but in your thinking be mature' (1 Cor. 14:20).

Such mature thinking about ministry will reflect on and embrace the Biblical reality that all our activity is commissioned and authenticated by Christ alone and that the glory of God is to be the servant's single focus and supreme concern. We need often to meditate on the verses which follow, so that they become written on our hearts and so dominate our ministry mind-set.

Jesus said, 'I am the vine; you are the branches. Whoever abides in me and I in him, he it is that bears much fruit, for apart from me you can do nothing' (John 15:5). 'All that the Father gives me will come to me, and whoever comes to me I will never cast out' (John 6:37). 'No one can come to me unless the Father who sent me draws him. And I will raise him up on the last day' (John 6:44). 'You did not choose me, but I chose you and appointed you that you should go and bear fruit and that your fruit should abide, so that whatever you ask the Father in my name, he may give it to you' (John 15:16). With such promises as these, who can doubt the strategic significance of a humble, dependent teaching ministry? It is as we devote ourselves to the content of Scripture, in order to preach its message to the thought patterns of our contemporary world, that we can ask the Holy Spirit's aid to make the connection with our hearers in life-changing ways.

It must be the Scriptures that are front and centre in ministry. Only then will our preaching accord with God's priorities and be used in bringing about God-honouring transformation.

4.

Preaching the transformational intention

Expository preaching can be described as preaching which takes the Biblical text so seriously that it shapes and controls the whole sermon. The text is in the driving seat. The text is king. But that can easily lead us to think that if we have exegeted the text and laid out its meaning to the congregation the preacher's job is done. In that case there would be no real difference between preaching and lecturing. The church building becomes an academic classroom and while the hearers' note books may be filled, their lives remain largely unaffected, unchanged. This is a pitfall for young preachers, straight out of seminary, who have been attending exegetical classes and writing academic essays, with multiple footnotes, for the past several years. Now they enter a pulpit to speak to real people facing multiple life situations in the real world. It can take some time for the seminary graduate to transition to being a pastor-teacher, but experience is a good mentor. As one disappointed listener said to me about his new, young pastor, 'All the application we ever get is "he who has ears to hear, let him hear".'

However, application is perhaps the most dangerous part of the whole exercise of preparing and preaching a Bible passage. All the hard work on exegesis is commendable, indeed vital, if the right applications are to be made. The whole process of preparation engages the preacher not only in working out what the preaching text means, but also what it signifies. A surface reading can provide much of the meaning, but you have to dig deeper for significance and that is what will produce effective application. The significance questions move us beyond 'what does the passage say?' to 'why does it say it?' And this in turn broadens out into other related questions, such as 'why does it say it in <u>these</u> terms?', 'why to <u>these</u> readers?' and 'why here at <u>this</u> point in the book and indeed in the whole revelation of the Bible?' Obviously, these questions are moving us towards application, because they are seeking to discover the intention of the writing, not just in terms of information, but with a view to potential life-change. That is why application is dangerous. It is at this stage that wrong ideas and fanciful notions can start to seep into the sermon, because the preacher is beginning to impose his own structural frameworks on the text. That can be as misleading and distorting as failure to interpret the meaning of the verses.

Preaching like that cuts against the grain of the passage, in order to emphasise the particular concerns or passions that the preacher has – the bees that are buzzing in his bonnet. But that is impository preaching, not expository. It becomes agenda preaching and starts to major on the 'ought to' applications, or the 'are we?' applications, which the preacher is wanting to lay upon his long-suffering hearers. 'We ought to be evangelising more.' 'Are we praying enough?' 'We ought to be giving more.' 'Are we growing in godliness?' Please do not misunderstand me. All of those things may be excellent and our hearers may need to be encouraged to act on them, but preaching that imposes my list of requirements on my hearers is subject to the law of diminishing returns. The more it happens, the more the congregation learns to recognise the familiar drum-beating and politely turn a deaf ear. Moreover, the overall effect is depressing, energy-sapping and demotivating, because it is the pressure of the preacher and his agenda, rather than the power of God's Word, which is being applied.

The careful expositor will want his preaching to be governed not only by the meaning of the text under consideration, but also and equally by its purpose. He recognises that God's Word is never given simply to teach its truth for us to file it away as mental knowledge, but always to make clear to us how we are to live in the light of that truth and also to reveal the spiritual dynamic by which such change becomes possible. Application is built into the text and the discovery of its practical purpose is as vital a part of our submission to the Word as is its careful exegesis. During the process of preparation we need to give time to articulating the theme sentence of the sermon, which is what we must preach from this unique text if we are to be faithful to its given content. But we also need to give time to working out our aim sentence, which is what we are praying God will be pleased to bring about in our own lives, and those of our hearers, as the purpose of the text is translated into our minds, hearts and wills. That must reflect its original purpose, which will be practical and pastoral; teaching, reproving, correcting and training in righteousness (2 Tim. 3:16). I want to call this the 'transformational intention' of the passage.

I am indebted to my friends, Todd Kelly and Tim Sattler, at WordPartners[1] for this descriptive term, which they suggested in our discussions about application, when we were working together on training programmes for expository preachers. What I particularly value is the expectation that is built in to the word 'transformational'. It's a note which I think is all too easily lost by Bible teachers. What was the Bible writer expecting to happen as a result of the text he is recording? What am I prayerfully expecting will be the result of my working at the text's original purpose, in order to see its intended transformation operating in my context today? Unless these concerns are the regular substance of our preparation, our preaching will always fall short of its aim, 'to present everyone mature in Christ'.

Because of our western individualism we are most likely to think of personal application to ourselves, first of all (which is good), and then to the other individuals who make up our congregation. We easily overlook the fact that most of the New Testament was written to church communities and even the personal letters were to be read to the churches. A major part of the transformational intention of the apostolic letters is that the churches should better understand, critique and so develop their own tasks and responsibilities. This is directed to their own cultural context of entrenched and growing hostile unbelief.

One of the weaknesses of contemporary evangelical preaching is that it often tends to operate within a 'bubble'

1. See their website for many excellent training materials at www.wordpartners.org

of Christian activity, which has only tangential connections with the world outside and its culture. Of course, it is much easier and less demanding for our preaching to remain confined to the life experience of me, as an individual, or my family, or my church, or my denomination. I am not denying for one moment that it is important for these concerns to be addressed, but I am suggesting that we need a much wider vision in application. And I wonder if some of our experience of being on the back foot in our culture is due to deficiencies of transformational intention in our preaching. If we are not being equipped by the preaching to go back into the world to fight the good fight twenty-four/ seven, all through the week, then we shall not be wanting to engage with the multiple challenges that are constantly thrown up by atheistic secularism. Church will then tend to become a self-indulgent retreat from everyday life and the 'bubble' will become increasingly introverted and less and less able to connect with our neighbours in ways that make a difference.

On reflection, I wonder too whether this may, at least partially, account also for the alarming wastage of children and young people from many churches. If the adults, who are the parents, teachers and leaders of the young, are not being equipped to be transformers in the home, at work, or in the social environment, through learning and practising the transformational intention of Scripture, they will pass on a one-dimensional, desiccated version of the faith to the next generation, which will fail lamentably to meet the urgent contemporary cultural challenges. If children are only taught a simplified version of the faith, like a sticking plaster for the wounds of life, the day will

come (perhaps quite soon) when they decide that this isn't
really worth bothering with and begin to make their exit.
They need to know that there is far more to discover in
the Bible and that the faith has far deeper and stronger
intellectual foundations and cultural application than they
have begun to understand, or even imagine. But they won't
know it if the adults are not themselves being taught it in
the preaching on Sunday. Part of the glory of Scripture
is that through the agency of divine revelation we have
the transformational tools to understand God's infallible
assessment of this world and so to demythologise its lies
and distortions. But that will not happen automatically.
We shall need to address both contexts of life, the church
and the culture, as we seek to activate the transformational
purposes within God's Word.

However, if our teaching is to fulfil this ultimate transformative goal, we need to be clear about the centrality of
the concept to God's purposes and the means by which
He teaches us to expect their fulfilment. A key text here is
2 Cor. 3:18, where Paul affirms, 'And we all, with unveiled
face, beholding the glory of the Lord, are being transformed
into the same image from one degree of glory to another.
For this comes from the Lord who is the Spirit.' In the
context of the letter, Paul is defending the validity of his
apostolic ministry, which he does by drawing attention to its
transformative power in the lives of the believers at Corinth,
which can only be attributed to the work of the Holy
Spirit. In its more immediate context, Paul is developing
his argument about the glories of the new covenant (3:6-8),
not of the letter of the law which kills, but of the Spirit
who gives life. There are two sets of comparisons operating

here. One is the contrast between the hardened minds of the Israelites (3:13-14) and the responsive hearts of the believers at Corinth. The other is between Moses and Paul, where the emphasis is on their similarity rather than their difference, for they both had their encounter with the God of glory, on Mount Sinai and on the road to Damascus.

As a result of Moses speaking with God his face shone with the reflected glory, so much so that Aaron and the people were afraid to come near him. So Moses veiled his face, except when he went in to the presence of the Lord to speak face to face (Exod. 34:29-35). The veil was lifted from Moses and the glory was seen in his face; he was transformed. Paul's point is that for the new covenant believer, the same encounter with the divine glory is the means of transformation and that this removal of the veil ('with unveiled face') is the work of the Holy Spirit, so that we can 'behold the glory of the Lord'. But that is the gift of God, who 'has shone in our hearts to give the light of the knowledge of the glory of God in the face of Jesus Christ' (2 Cor. 4:6). For Christians, the Spirit replaces our hearts of stone with hearts of flesh (Ezek. 36:26), opens our unbelieving minds, blinded by the god of this world (2 Cor. 4:4) and endows us with the freedom to understand and believe the gospel (v. 17). It is with opened eyes that we behold the glory of the Lord Jesus and are being transformed into His image. But how can we see His glory, other than in the Scriptures? Verse 15 speaks about 'reading Moses' but for Israel 'a veil lies over their hearts' and for all humanity there is a blindness to the Lord and the gospel which we are not able to overcome. 'But when one turns to the Lord, the veil is removed. Now the Lord is the Spirit, and where the Spirit of the Lord is, there is freedom' (vv. 16-17). He brings freedom from hard-hearted unbelief and with it freedom to understand, believe and obey the gospel and begin to experience all its benefits.[2]

Transformation is the great benefit, which is the focus of verse 18. The change is that we become increasingly like the one on whom our faith focuses, 'transformed into the same image'. The evidence of this being real is not in the ecstatic experiences or spiritual mysticism which the Corinthians seem so much to have desired, but in character transformation, growing in godliness, becoming more and more like the Lord Jesus. The verb is in the present tense – 'we are being transformed'. The experience is progressive, 'from one degree of glory to another'. It begins when our minds and hearts are first opened to the good news of Christ and it will continue until its completion and fulfilment in the glory of the eternal Kingdom. 'We know that when he appears we shall be like him, because we shall see him as he is' (1 John 3:2). Already the image of God has been perfectly revealed in the person of Jesus the Word made flesh, and in His designation as the 'last Adam', He has perfectly fulfilled the Father's will in His faithful, total obedience. So He has become the head of a redeemed humanity, 'the firstborn among many brothers', who are being 'conformed to his image' (Rom. 8:29). 'And we all … are being transformed into the same image' (v. 18). It is this glorious work of the Spirit, uplifting and glorifying the Lord Jesus, taking all that belongs to

---

2. For a detailed and stimulating study of this passage; see 'Paul, Moses and the History of Israel,' by Scott J. Hafemann; Hendrickson, Peabody MA, 1996; Chapter 5, pp. 363-426.

Christ and declaring it to His people and to the world, as He convicts of sin and righteousness and judgment (John 16:13-14), which is our constant motivation to keep teaching the whole revelation of God, in all the Scriptures, since this is the means of God's transformational grace.

In our communities, there is an urgent need to return to, and be motivated by, the shape, priorities and spiritual purposes of the church as expounded by the teaching of Jesus and the apostles. The salt of the earth, the light of the world, the city set on a hill (Matt. 5:13-14) are all images that define intentionality. The concerns that the apostles have for the well-being of the churches, which we shall examine elsewhere, will move us away from the success syndrome and the maximisation of numbers and resources, which can so easily lead to a church being run like a strand of God's commercial enterprise. 'Do not be conformed to this world, but be transformed by the renewal of your mind, that by testing you may discern what is the will of God, what is good and acceptable and perfect' (Rom. 12:2). Transformation is central to authorial intention throughout the epistles. This is the pre-requisite if we are to be able to live according to God's will in a broken world. Without the transforming power of the Word to make the church fit for purpose, we shall never realise how deeply the spirit of the age has invaded, colonised and now dominates large sections of corporate church life.

In his 1993 book, 'The Fabric of Theology', Richard Lints both identified and foresaw three particular cultural influences or emphases, where the New Testament

challenges the church to radical transformation.[3] What
he warned against nearly thirty years ago has only become
more powerful and destructive in the intervening time.
First, he identifies pluralism, by which the whole world is
brought into our living rooms on a constant daily basis. In
1993 it was via the TV news channels, but just consider
the avalanche of social media information (true and
false), comment and opinion today. Pluralism has become
the only acceptable norm, which is an irony in itself.
But once the objective existence of truth in the form of
absolute standards has been rejected and the very concept
rubbished, the church is under immense pressure about its
message and raison d'etre.

The church will never be able to function effectively as
salt and light if it begins to move from the ultimately total
authority of God's infallible Word. Her very existence
depends upon an authoritative message from God, to
proclaim and live by and that is unique because it is the only
authority claim that is rooted outside of human authority
and opinion. Of course, we recognise that claiming divine
authority for the Bible does not prove it to be so, but all
the competing authority claims, whether in the culture or
when they are adopted by the church, are constrained by
finite and temporal human judgments. If the Bible is not
our ultimate ground of authority we shall inevitably turn
to our own reason, or to our cultural traditions, or (and
especially today) our own experience. If it feels good, it is
good. If I think something is or should be so, then that
establishes that it must be. So, contemporary preachers

---

3. 'The Fabric of Theology,' Richard Lints; Eerdmans, Grand Rapids;
   1993.

succumb to the temptation to downplay or de-emphasise the Bible's teaching wherever it is thought to be 'divisive'. Evil, sin, judgment, hell – they all begin to be eased out of the public utterance, to be replaced by a God who becomes a sort of spiritual Santa Claus, where the emphasis will be on what he can give you and do for you, because you are special. So, as Lints observes, people say, 'How can there be a God, if we are not happy all the time?'

Secondly, he identifies the cult of the self as a dominant focus. Peter Berger summed it up as the movement from 'fate' to 'choice'. And this has only mushroomed over the years. Our culture tells us that we can be in control of our own destinies. We can be whatever we want to be, whoever we want to be, whether in terms of gender and sexuality, body image or personal identity. Life has become about maximising your personal happiness, providing you are not causing harm to others by restricting their individual choices. Pop psychology and the self-help and fulfilment ethos seem to be entrenched in many churches and Christians.

However, another Christian writer, Larry Crabb, made similar observations back in 1988 in his title 'Inside Out', more recently revised and updated,[4] in which the introductory chapter is headed 'The False Hope of Modern Christianity'. He identifies the false hope as the teaching that 'an inexpressible joy is available that rather than support us through hard times can actually eliminate pressure, worry and pain from our experience.' He continues, 'Orthodox Bible preachers ... appeal to that

---

4. 'Inside Out,' by Larry Crabb; Nav Press in alliance with Tyndale House Publishers, 2013; pp. 27-29.

same desire for relief from groaning. They tell us that more knowledge, more commitment, more giving, more prayer—some combination of Christian disciplines—will eliminate our need to struggle with deeply felt realities'. Wanting now what the Bible tells us can only be ours in the perfect world to come, leads to a life of make-believe and pretence, which has a devastating effect both on the church and the world. Crabb concludes, 'The effect of widespread pretense, whether maintained by rigidly living on the surface of life or being consumed with emotionalism, has been traumatic for the church. Rather than being salt and light, we've become a theologically diverse community of powerless Pharisees, penetrating very little of society because we refuse to grapple honestly with the experience of life.' The whole book has some profound challenges to preachers about the proper application of Scripture to Christian living, working with the transformational intention inherent in the text.

The third weakness Lints alerts us to is the cult of simplicity. Over and over again I have heard the mnemonic KISS used to describe the nature of effective preaching – 'Keep it simple, stupid'. I have to say that it is often an excuse for superficial thinking and shoddy preparation. Of course, there is no virtue in complexity for its own sake, but to reduce everything to the lowest common denominator of simplicity is likely to produce a church of 'children, tossed to and fro by the waves and carried about by every wind of doctrine, by human cunning, by craftiness in deceitful schemes' (Eph. 4:14). It will certainly not produce strongly-rooted maturing believers who are growing up into Christ. Clarity in preaching is not the same as being simplistic. As Richard Lints says, 'Don't aim for ease, but for depth.' Preaching that merely strings together sound bites and slogans, with a few emotional stories will be in danger of presenting a Jesus who is a marketable package to benefit you – a spiritual product you really ought to sample. Evangelism then becomes sales talks, mechanistic and technique-oriented, choosing the market and going for the deal. But the transformational intention of Scripture is to produce a Christian mind, which develops a Christian world-view, so that the whole of life is conditioned and controlled by God's truth and is a coherent response to His Word.

It is a rule of Biblical instruction that the indicatives must precede the imperatives. The teaching must precede the demands. The reason for this is that the commands of Scripture all flow from the teaching content, as they are the application of the implications within the passage. The transformational intention is directly derived from the teaching content. When that does not happen, the applications that are imposed will nearly always lead either to legalism or to licence, which is why Christians and churches remain weak. The reason is that when the imperatives are imposed, rather than drawn out from the text, while they may be received enthusiastically enough, we quickly come to realise that we cannot carry them out. Either we decide that we must put in more effort and commit ourselves to the cold duty of striving to obey the rules and regulations we are under, or we decide we can't do them and we don't need to.

The way of legalism will tend to produce either a proud Pharisee, who wants to present as a perfect rule-keeper, but who inevitably has to hide failures and so turns into a play-acting hypocrite, or else a deflated defeatist

endlessly looking within to see why he cannot live up to
the standards his Pharisee brothers seem to be achieving.
The way of licence tends to reject all instruction, even the
plain commands of Scripture, and ends up with a careless
attitude to life and to God, where I can basically do as I
like, because God understands and it is His business to
forgive. As preachers, we need to be much more aware of the
negative knock-on effects which imposing our applications
on our hearers, rather than showing them persuasively the
implications of the text, can produce in people's lives.

Remember that in Scripture the transformational
intention is not always in the imperative mode. Think how
often the Lord Jesus used the interrogative, to stimulate
engagement with His teaching. For example, Matthew's
accounts of the parable of the lost sheep (18:12) and that
of the two sons sent to work in the vineyard (21:28) are
preceded by Jesus' words, 'What do you think?' He doesn't
merely want His hearers to listen to the parable, but to
engage with its teaching, to think it through for themselves.
Similarly in Luke 10:36, at the end of the parable of the
Good Samaritan, Jesus asks the lawyer, 'Which of these
three, do you think, proved to be a neighbour to the
man who fell among robbers?' Many times, during His
ministry, a miraculous action or a piece of teaching begins
with a question by which Jesus clearly intends to involve
those with whom He is dealing, not just in listening to a
proclamation from Him, but engaging their own thought
processes, so that what is said or done is never merely
external to them. Instead, they are caught up in thinking
through the implications of what they are witnessing and
applying them to their own internal and personal lives.

There are surely important clues here as to how we might make our own teaching of the transformational intention of a passage more effective. We need to follow Jesus' example in encouraging our hearers to think through the implications of the verses we are preaching. This is the ministry of the Holy Spirit, the 'paraclete' as Jesus described him, the one who is called alongside to help. It is the picture of the teacher coming alongside young children who are just learning to form their letters. They have a model to follow both in the example of the perfectly finished letter presented to them and by seeing how the teacher produced it. But what a difference it makes when the teacher puts her hand over the child's hand and gently guides the pencil and shapes the letter, so that the child gets the feel of how to do it and is able, by practice, to internalise the methodology and make it their own. This is the teacher's role in preaching too, evidenced in the number of times Luke uses the verb 'persuade', in his account of apostolic ministry in the book of Acts. As we try to help our hearers to work through the transformational intention of the passage being preached, questions bring the preacher's presentation alongside the hearer's thinking to persuade them to action. 'What do you think?' 'Do you see how this might work out for you?' 'If you were to act on this could this be the outcome, could these be the benefits?' 'This is how it worked in someone else's life (perhaps directly in the text, or in a contemporary illustration) now, how about you?' 'Don't you want to travel that way too?'

Please note, we are not trying to control our hearers. There is nothing overbearing about such an approach and we are certainly not wanting to shape our hearers into our own image. But we do want our preaching to move not just from the text to the sermon, but from the text to life. Congregations are not passive buckets into which information needs to be pumped. Like us, they are 'becomers', with a long way to go, many questions to be answered and many issues to be resolved, but what an enormous privilege for the preacher to be used by God, as the Word is expounded, to be an agent of transformation!

Transformational intention then must be an essential part of our preaching. We need to be working hard to understand the pastoral purpose with which the passage was written and then showing the implications of its truth for our hearers. Application must flow from the text rather than being bolted on by the preacher. Failure to do this will result in stunted growth, a Christianity abstracted from the real world and an arbitrary list of do this more and do this less. It will cultivate a superficial thought life in the Christian and a weak faith that will be easily swamped by the challenges of real life in a fallen world. However, preaching the transformational intention of each passage will lead to growth, vibrancy and robustness in our hearers as they live as thinking Christians in a hostile world.

5.

Preaching to cultivate a robust faith in a shifting world

'Faith', according to the cynic, 'is believing what you know isn't true'. That put-down is everywhere in our contemporary culture. It opposes faith to rationality and implies that those who resort to it are either woefully ignorant, or wilfully resistant to the plain facts of life on planet Earth, evidenced all around us. Built on the enlightenment concept that the only certain realities are those which we can observe through our physical senses and which are therefore open to scientific investigation, the arguments against faith want to locate its origin within the person of the believer. The classic example might be that of the French philosopher-mathematician La Place, who when asked by Napoleon why his book on astronomy contained no reference to God replied, 'Sir, I have no need of that hypothesis'. After two hundred years, that attitude epitomises so much of our modern world. God is at best an hypothesis, or merely a figment of the imagination, not worthy of serious consideration by intelligent materialists who inhabit the 'real' world.

In total contrast, for the Christian believer, 'faith' is the key component of one's life and experience. However, the

all-important difference is that Christian faith does not find
its origin in the believer, so it is not generated by the will or
the emotions. Rather, it is in itself a response to the objective
realities of God's self-revelation, in the world of time and
space, through the events and explanations of history. At
first sight, we might seem to be entirely on the back foot
in our preaching when we call people to faith, but actually
we are calling them to certainties in the unseen, yet more
real, context of the God who made, controls and governs
all things, according to His own sovereign will. We need
therefore to explore the rationale of faith, not only to answer
the critics on their own ground, but also to encourage those
to whom we preach to realise that no surrender of their
critical faculties is needed to have faith in God.

However, our current situation is somewhat more
complex than this because the inadequacies and failure
of the rationalist system have become increasingly
clear throughout the world. Political disillusionment
is widespread, but that is perhaps only a symptom of a
deeper malaise, seen in our universities and public forum,
on a constant daily basis, across the globe. Writing as long
ago as 1986 James M. Boice could already identify the
root of the problem when reason is taken as the ultimate
authority. 'It can tell us what is, but it cannot tell us what
ought to be. Consequently, the extraordinary technical
advances of our time are accompanied by an extreme and
debilitating moral permissiveness which promises in time
to break down even the values and system that made both
the advances and the permissiveness possible.'[1] In the

1. 'Foundations of the Christian Faith,' by J. M. Boice; IVP, 1986,
   Leicester; p. 20.

years that have followed we have witnessed an increasing abandonment of rationalism for the mysticism of eastern religion, the addiction of 'recreational' drugs, the hedonism of the self-indulgent 'me' culture, the quest for experience of whatever sort and at whatever price. Much of this may well be a reaction against Reason (with the capital 'R' to show its pretension to control and dominate), but how are we as preachers to tackle those challenges?

The God of the Bible is by definition transcendent. *The Pocket Oxford English Dictionary* (1969) defines the verb to transcend as 'to be or pass beyond the range of, be too high for, soar above, surpass (experience, comprehension, competition, limitations, etc.)', which is a fine theological definition of the nature of God, supreme over His creation and distinct from it. His invisibility contributes to our understanding of the situation. He is not God at the end of a string, or under a microscope. We are not in a position to demand anything from such a being who is omniscient, omnipotent, infinite and eternal, totally self-sufficient. If we are ever to have a truthful, real apprehension of Him, He must disclose Himself to us and it is reasonable to suppose that were this to happen it would be in some unique revelation of His character and will, yet in terms that could be readily understood by the whole human race. The central claim of Christianity is that this has indeed happened, in the self-revelation of God in the real man in real history who is Jesus Christ. This is not some faith statement or concept which originates in the believer, but is actually both a rational and emotional response to the evidence presented externally in the objective historical record. So, the Christian position is that faith, far from being a 'leap in the dark', is a conviction, leading to action, on the basis of the objective evidence of what God has done objectively historically.

This, then, gives us a potential point of contact, which is seized on by the apostle Paul in Romans 10:13-17 where he expounds the means by which faith in Christ is generated. Salvation comes from calling on the name of the Lord (v. 13). But men will not call if they do not believe, and they will not believe if they have not heard, and they will not hear unless someone preaches (v. 14). The famous summary of verse 17 is foundational to all our efforts in proclamation. 'So faith comes from hearing and hearing through the word of Christ.' Christ's person and work reveal both the true nature of God and the way to become part of His eternal kingdom, but we can only encounter Him when we hear the word of the gospel, both in the pages of Scripture and in its faithful proclamation by the people of God. Paul makes the same point when he describes the Ephesian Christians as having 'learned Christ'. How did that happen? 'You have heard about him and were taught in him, as the truth is in Jesus' (Eph. 4:20-21). You heard; you were taught; you learned. Biblical Christian experience focuses on hearing, not seeing. Indeed, the apostolic testimony is that 'we walk by faith, not by sight' (2 Cor. 5:7).

But that is counter-intuitive, because we want to see where we are going; we want to be able to apprehend reality with our senses and to analyse it with our minds. God's kingly rule, however, is an invisible reality, which spreads by the proclamation of the gospel, but which exists in a totally different dimension from normal human sensual perception. So Jesus teaches the Pharisees, 'The kingdom of God is not coming in ways that can be observed, nor will they say, "Look, here it is!" or "There!" for behold, the kingdom of God is in the midst of you' (Luke 17:20-21). This might equally be translated 'within you', or 'within your grasp' (ESV footnotes), but the point of the saying is the hiddenness of the reality of the kingdom of God to those who depend only on the human resources of their senses. Was this a major cause of the fall back in Genesis 3? The serpent's tactic in tempting Eve is to cast doubts on the dependability of what God has said, to undermine and so attack His character. 'Did God actually say, "You shall not eat of any tree in the garden?"' (Gen. 3:1). This insinuation progresses to a denial of its validity and therefore of God's dependability. 'You will not surely die' (v. 4). But the action of the fall is triggered by what is visible. 'When the woman saw that the tree was good for food, and that it was a delight to the eyes, and that the tree was to be desired to make one wise, she took of its fruit and ate, and she also gave some to her husband who was with her, and he ate' (v. 6). The choice is to walk by sight and not by faith in the good character of God as revealed in His Word.

The same wrong direction is corrected by Jesus Himself, in the famous narrative of doubting (better unbelieving) Thomas in John 20. The chapter centres on the relationship between sight and faith, in terms of the historical fact of Christ's resurrection and its world-changing implications. 'Seeing is believing' seems, at first, to be the heart of the message. Peter and John discover the empty tomb, which they both enter and John testifies that 'he *saw* and believed' (v. 8). Mary Magdalene meets the risen Lord in the garden and announces to the disciples, 'I have *seen* the Lord'

(v. 18). Jesus visits the disciples on Easter evening, showing them His hands and His side. 'Then the disciples were glad when they *saw* the Lord' (v. 20). But Thomas, who was not present, later protests, 'Unless I *see* in his hands the mark of the nails ... I will never believe' (v. 25). This is so true to human experience and at one level not at all unreasonable. Even the disciples dismissed the testimony of the women although they had seen the tomb was empty and heard the angel's message, 'He is not here, but has risen'. To them, at first, it seemed to be 'an idle tale and they did not believe them' (Luke 24:10-11). In his account, John inserts the comment that 'as yet they did not understand the Scripture, that he must rise from the dead' (John 20:9). The implication is that the word of resurrection promise, which Jesus had given them on several occasions, coupled with the Old Testament prophecy should have been the object of their faith and sufficient for their assurance.

But Jesus does appear to Thomas. He is able to see and to touch and as he does so to fulfil Jesus' exhortation, 'Do not disbelieve, but believe' (John 20:27), he declares his response to Jesus, 'My Lord and my God' (v. 28). The apostles, who are the witnesses of the reality of the resurrection, commissioned by the risen Lord to be His ambassadors, needed to have the evidence presented to them as a reality in time and space, apprehended through their senses. But that was not to be the normal pattern. How could it be when Jesus had returned to the Father and the good news of His kingly rule was rapidly spreading across the Mediterranean world? 'Have you believed because you have seen me?' Jesus asks Thomas. 'Blessed are those who have not seen and yet have believed' (v. 29). Faith now depends on the apostles' word of eye-witness testimony, on learning Christ through the apostolic preaching and in documents such as John's Gospel, 'written so that you may believe that Jesus is the Christ, the Son of God, and that by believing you may have life in his name' (v. 31). We believe because they saw and testified. 'So faith comes from hearing, and hearing through the word of Christ' (Rom. 10:17).

There is a helpful addition to our understanding this priority from the life of Martin Luther and his theology of the cross. In his book 'A Cloud of Witnesses', Prof Alister McGrath describes how Luther developed the gospel accounts of the crucifixion in terms of the hidden reality of what was happening as Jesus died, which was in direct contrast with what those present at the event would have perceived through their senses. To them it must have seemed as though God was either absent, or inactive. But such a view was transformed by the resurrection, which demonstrated that God was in fact both present and active, but hidden. Luther used this to show that judgments based on human perception or experience cannot come to any reliable assessment of the activity of the unseen God. McGrath comments, 'For Luther, the resurrection demonstrates the superiority of faith in the promises of God over reliance upon experience or reason. We must learn to let God be God, and trust in him and his promises, rather than in our own finite and inadequate perception of a situation.'[2]

The theological and practical implications of this are profound for the preacher who wants to be faithful to both

2. 'A Cloud of Witnesses,' by A. E. McGrath; IVP Leicester, 1990; pp. 64-65.

the contents and the methodology of Biblical teaching and gospel proclamation. The big danger is that we may lose confidence in the proclamation of the Word of God and in its unique power and ability to accomplish God's purposes. Our propensity then is gradually to drift from hearing the word of Christ towards looking at visual images about Christianity. We live in a predominantly visual culture, where we are bombarded with visual images all our waking hours. Our imaginations are largely stimulated by what we see, whether in the sophisticated and powerful persuasion of the advertisers, or the innumerable selfies and visual images sent across social media from our ubiquitous phones. And this is not to mention the amazing graphics that can simulate an entire virtual universe. We want to live by sight, rather than faith. It's more immediate, more exciting, more real, more rewarding – or so we imagine.

Evangelical Christians are not immune to such dominant cultural pressures – far from it. In fact there is a continually growing demand for visible images to take over from the preached word as the most successful 'bridge' into the secular culture of our times. 'A picture is worth a thousand words', we are told. But that depends on what the thousand words are, what they are conveying and what they are designed to do. It also depends upon the veracity of the visual image. 'The camera does not lie' they say; but camera angles, what is the focus in the frame and what is deliberately excluded, along with the contemporary skills of 'touching up' a visual image can all contribute to the distortion of the reality. The image is designed to produce an immediate impression, usually emotionally driven, but not to provide material for detailed thought or investigation. However, such immediacy is also the mother of transience. It's always on to the next one and how many do we ever remember? Some preachers seem to spend as much if not more time looking for great video clips to illustrate their sermons, than they do on careful study of the Word of God. But which will have the lasting, life-changing impact?

We must not lose our nerve, or to quote Paul, in 2 Corinthians 4:1 and 16, 'we do not lose heart'. Paul's concluding reason at the end of that chapter on apostolic priorities is that 'we look not to the things that are seen but to the things that are unseen. For the things that are seen are transient, but the things that are unseen are eternal' (2 Cor. 4:18). If the ultimate, eternal realities with which the gospel deals are unseen, then faith can only be generated by God's spoken word, not by our reflection on the sensory experiences we might want to call 'spiritual'. Those could be a response to beautiful images, uplifting music, even emotional stories in preaching, but do they generate 'faith', and if they do, what is the object of that faith? It is all too easy to put our faith in faith, which without clear verbal and objective content will always tend towards the indulgence of warm feelings and emotional gratification. That is no foundation to withstand life's storms. True Christian experience of God, which is what we should all long for more and more, must be dictated and guaranteed by the God who speaks His Word. In other words, it is the product of faith and always has been from the very beginning.

Abraham, the supreme example of faith in the Old Testament, responds to the initiative which God takes to bring him into a personal relationship. God's commissioning Word is full of promise and grace – to make of Abraham a great nation, to bless him and make his name great, to bless all the families of the earth in him, and to provide him with a land to live in. With the promise comes a command, 'Go from your country and your kindred and your father's house to the land that I will show you' (Gen. 12:1-3). This undeserved favour of God, expressed in the promises, produces in Abraham the trust and confidence, which enable him to obey – to venture out into the unknown with God. 'And he believed the LORD, and he counted it to him as righteousness' (Gen. 15:6). That led Abraham to a life-time of experiencing God, as his faith grew and deepened as he progressed towards spiritual maturity.

Speaking of the long years of waiting for the fulfilment of the promise in the birth of his son, Isaac, the apostle Paul gives us this insight. 'No distrust made him waver concerning the promise of God, but he grew strong in his faith as he gave glory to God, fully convinced that God was able to do what he had promised' (Rom. 4:20-21). It is striking that it was his perception of God that kept him persevering, and so growing in faith. He didn't distrust God ... he was 'fully convinced' God would keep His promise. It wasn't even that he simply believed the promise, but rather that he trusted the God who made the promise. Faith is a relational response of the whole person to the living God, as He reveals Himself through His living and enduring Word.

If we want our preaching ministry to raise maturing Christians, who are men and women of growing faith, then we need to return to the Biblical conviction that faith is a gift of God. Paul makes the point, almost incidentally, when he reminds the Philippians that 'it has been granted to you that for the sake of Christ you should not only believe in him, but also suffer for his sake' (Phil. 1:29). Believing in Christ is 'granted to you'. Faith is God's gift, as Ephesians 2:8-9 declares with even greater intentionality. The vocabulary stresses the evidence of God's undeserved favour (grace) and kindness, freely given. Faith is not something that we can generate, either within ourselves or our hearers. God sovereignly decrees to grant the gift of faith, but we know that the agency He uses is the preaching of the Word of Christ (Rom. 10:17). So that is our responsibility, both in terms of faithful content and persevering practice. But in the preceding chapter of Romans, Paul has already established the sovereignty of God in granting salvation. Citing Exod 33:19, where God says to Moses, 'I will have mercy on whom I have mercy and I will have compassion on whom I have compassion', Paul affirms, 'So then it depends not on human will or exertion, but on God who has mercy' (Rom. 9:15-16).

It seems to me that this Biblical understanding should have much deeper significance and wider ramifications for our preaching than we commonly recognise. In our fiercely secular context, we all realise that there is a huge mountain to climb if the multitudes of unbelieving people all around us are to hear the gospel. A handful may be in each of our churches week by week, but what are they among so many? How are we to reach the millions who are currently outside of any effective gospel witness? Of course, that is a right question to ask, since we follow a Saviour who wept

over Jerusalem and its rejection of His salvation at the
time of His visitation. If we know anything of the realities
of heaven and hell, we shall be passionate to see as many
as possible coming to experience God's gracious rescue.
That will keep us preaching and witnessing and above all
praying. But if we are not totally persuaded that salvation,
while by faith alone and in Christ alone, is also by grace
alone, it is likely that we shall be diverted into what will
effectively become a preaching cul-de-sac, with disastrous
effects on the life of our churches. Indeed this is evidently
happening already in some churches in our own context.

How are we to reach more of those who are not at all
within the orbit of our churches? The obvious answer would
seem to be to deploy all of our church members as much more
active evangelists. We might do that in two main ways. First
we could run training courses within our churches to equip
everyone for this task. They would have several different
focal points. Obviously, it would be important to teach
everybody what the Biblical gospel is and to provide them
with relevant Scripture passages to convey its truth. Then
we might have practical training about how to build bridges
to non-Christian colleagues, friends, neighbours and family,
how to initiate conversations and how to answer questions
and objections. That, in turn, may require some additional
training in basic apologetics. All of this can be extremely
valuable, and I am not at all wanting to be negative about it.
But we have to face the reality that we have been doing this
for many years now in our churches and it doesn't seem to
be having a positive effect as widespread as we would love
to see. Our churches are still quite introverted, generally,
and while there are some wonderful exceptions many of us

seem to find it difficult to make the connections. There are some who are already gifted evangelists, evidenced by the fact that others are coming to Christ through them on a regular basis. We praise God for them, longing and praying that He would raise up more. But many of our members are elderly and lacking the energy they once had. Or, those younger are tied down by demands of work, family and church responsibilities so that time to build bridges to unbelievers is very limited and extra energy is at a premium. Younger people may be busy at their studies or daunted by the scepticism all around them and decide that a private faith and going low profile are the best tactics for survival.

So, secondly, we decide to make evangelism the major ingredient of our preaching menu. There is a mantra which says, 'the gospel in every sermon', but the danger is that we interpret this to mean 'only the gospel in every sermon'. Now of course this depends on how we define 'the gospel'. If we take it to be a synonym for the whole counsel of God, then what else would we be preaching anyway? But if we follow the contemporary trends which downgrade the congregation's ability to deal with anything other than a simplistic presentation (family services all the time) and favour the exhortation 'Keep it simple, stupid', then a considerable part of our regular preaching becomes entry level Christianity at its most basic. 'The hungry sheep look up and are not fed', John Milton lamented in his poem 'Lycidas' (1637) and that was in Puritan England. Nearly 400 years later, those of us who stand on the same theological convictions are in danger of seeing the sheep as reluctant evangelists who have to be exhorted or cajoled into action, to the point that many of our sermons tend towards the same conclusion, to go out there and evangelize. In Spurgeon's day he chided those preachers of whom he said, 'Ten thousand thousand are their texts, but all their sermons are one!'

Again, please do not misconstrue what I am trying to say. Evangelism is enormously important and I know from my own pastoral experience how hard it is to keep it at the top of our church's priorities. Equipping by training is a very important part of our church activity. But I wonder if we are in danger of forgetting that faith is God's gift and are drifting almost imperceptibly into what betrays itself ultimately as a man-centred rather than God-centred approach. This was the thrust of a seminal paper which was delivered as his Presidential Address for the UCCF in 1975, by William Still, who was minister of Gilcomston South Church, Aberdeen, Scotland from 1945 to 1997, retiring as the longest serving minister in the Church of Scotland on his 87th birthday. Known for his consecutive expository preaching of the whole Bible, chapter by chapter, he became a major exemplar and influence on decades of young preachers in Scotland and further afield. The thrust of his 1975 address, which traced what he saw as the decline from the Reformation and Puritan heritage to the evangelicalism of the 20th century, was to enquire how the changes happened and might be remedied. He wrote, 'The difference may be roughly characterised as a change in emphasis from the sovereignty of grace to appeal to the will of men; from God-centred religion to man-centred religion'.

In pursuing his thesis, William Still calls for 'a clear distinction' between the words 'evangelical' and 'evangelistic', which he articulates as follows: 'The distinction between the words as I see it is that whereas "evangelical" suggests a full and rounded use of the whole Bible, thoroughly evangelical in interpretation to build up the Church's life and witness until it overflows and reaches out to a needy world; "evangelistic" suggests a going out to the world with a message made applicable to the unconverted ("geared" is the modern word) and drawn from the corpus of the Bible.' Evangelism is not a mechanistic add-on to a Christian's duties but the overflow of the life of Christ within, through the Holy Spirit. Still concludes: 'There is no doubt that preoccupation with what is narrowly evangelistic tends to run to seed, to a seed which seeds its own death, because it exhausts itself ultimately with self-effort, and hardly retains strength or will enough to reproduce itself and therefore periodically has to whip itself up into extraordinary efforts to fulfil its evangelistic calling; whereas preoccupation with evangelical theology (as long as its doctrine remains biblical and spiritual and doesn't turn aside to one or other of the twin dangers of religiosity or legalism) leads to its own natural and normal outreach, in the cure and care of souls and in building a strong Church.'[3] That is a long sentence, but it is well worth pondering!

If we accept this thesis, it follows that the building up of Christians in maturity of godly character is the prior concern of the older evangelical theology over simply gaining new converts. Both matter; but the one will follow from the other. The Church is built as its members 'attain to the unity of the faith and of the knowledge of the

---

3. Presidential Address to UCCF (1975) – published privately by Gilcomston South Church, Aberdeen.

Son of God, to mature manhood, to the measure of the stature of the fulness of Christ ... from whom the whole body ... when each part is working properly, makes bodily growth so that it builds itself up in love' (Eph. 4:13-16). The fulness of Jesus will always overflow from individual believers, through a healthy church, to build up the body both in quality and then quantity – but in that order. A great deal depends, then, on how we see this sort of robust, grown-up faith being generated, whether in the initial work of the new birth or the ongoing life of the believer. It comes by preaching the whole counsel of God, because such life is God's gift, as the Spirit of God takes the Word of God to accomplish the work of God. And to that we must now turn.

6.

Preaching the whole truth

For many evangelical pastors and teachers, the area of Scripture we tend to inhabit most happily is the epistles of the New Testament. There are very good reasons for this. Not only do they exist in the same era of salvation-history as ourselves, that is between the first and second comings of our Lord Jesus, what the New Testament calls 'the last days'. But they are also written in the style of consecutive development of logical arguments, which is the intellectual thought-pattern in which we have been reared, as has the western church for centuries past. We must of course be careful to give adequate weight and importance to the other ingredients of Biblical revelation, such as Old Testament narrative, poetry, wisdom literature and apocalyptic, alongside the four Gospels, Acts and Revelation, so that over a period of time we develop a full-orbed ministry and preach the whole revelation of God. However, we are likely to find ourselves in the epistles over and over again. The doctrinal teaching is so concentrated and the ethical imperatives so practical. We are right, surely, to work hard here so that our hearers are fully instructed in this major genre of Biblical truth.

Yet it is easy to overlook the reason why the Lord chose to inspire the apostles to convey the developing revelation of Christian theology in this format. It is at least arguable that God might have inspired something much nearer to a comprehensive systematic theological text book, but He chose not to. This seems to be because all revealed truth is primarily relational. Scripture is full of propositional statements and objective truth about God, His purposes and requirements, of course, but never in a detached or impersonal way. We are right to affirm that the Bible is God preaching God to us, that it is His book about Himself before it is His book about us. But this is never merely 'knowledge', to be written in a note-book or filed away in a memory-bank. It is God opening a conversation with those who hear or read His word, designed to bring human beings into a deep personal relationship with Him. It requires a response of truth and obedience to develop a new centre of being, expressed as loving God with all one's heart, mind and strength, which is what Christian maturity is all about. Simply to filter out the doctrinal content, to separate it from the practical, transformational intention of the divinely-inspired message would be a serious distortion.

This insight has profound effects on our teaching and preaching method. It means that we cannot be content with delivering what is effectively a lecture on an aspect of systematic theology, extracted from the text, without asking those much harder questions about why this passage is here, at this point, in this letter, written to these people. Preaching the 'what does it say?' is a good and necessary beginning, but if we do not move further into the 'why?' questions our application (if there is any) will be contrived, bolted on and conditioned by the preacher's current personal emphases, rather than the author's divinely-inspired intention.

Undoubtedly, the equal and opposite danger is always present too and is the pit into which most of us fall only too easily. Knowing that we must be 'relevant', we rush to the application, paying scant attention to the original context and preach the imperatives of the passage without consideration of the essential, undergirding indicatives. Yet if we give more thought to the original purpose of the epistle it will protect us from the twin dangers of cold abstraction and imposed rule-making. The point is that the teaching content of the epistles is always related to the practical issues of living the Christian life, since it is the mistakes, errors, false trails and sheer rebellion of even the regenerate human heart that prompt the apostolic writers to expound and expand their readers' understanding of God's mind and will. All the teaching has direct life-application purpose.

Recognising this will perhaps give us some fresh insight into how to build the bridge from the text to our hearers more effectively. It is highly instructive and profitable to try to immerse ourselves more fully in the original apostolic concerns, which were themselves produced by the range of problems and challenges they encountered in the churches they served. So, drawing up a list of the major practical issues of Christian faith and life which the epistles address can be very enlightening for us, not just historically but pastorally. The reason why the Holy Spirit inspired and has preserved the apostolic writings of the New Testament is not simply historical or antiquarian.

Down the millennia the same issues have challenged the church time and time again. This is hardly surprising since if God does not change neither does human nature. The clothing and context may look different from one generation to the next, but the underlying issues remain the same. Even regenerate human nature faces the same challenges in every generation in engaging in the constant battle of the faith against the world, the flesh and the devil. 'The whole world lies in the power of the evil one' (1 John 5:19). To have divine instruction so accurately analytical of the issues at stake, coupled with the divine remedy in the truth of the gospel and its application to every area of life – these are the great resources and treasures of the apostolic deposit. 'For whatever was written in former days was written for our instruction, that through endurance and through the encouragement of the Scriptures we might have hope' (Rom. 15:4). Paul's thought here was about the Old Testament Scriptures, but his comment surely has equal relevance for the New Testament writings for us, two thousand years later. There is no yawning chasm between what the epistles were designed to accomplish for their original readers and their unchanging benefits to us today.

Perhaps a good place to start is the last in time of the letters written to first century churches, in chapters 2 and 3 of the book of Revelation. Whatever date we assign to John's 'prophecy' (1:3) it is clearly positioned towards the end of the apostolic era, as the baton is being passed to the next generation, which consists of those who have not seen and yet have believed (John 20:29). It is instructive firstly to identify what the churches are commended for, since these provide us with the qualities of godly living or spiritual maturity which the glorified Lord (1:12-16) looks for in His redeemed people.

The first letter, to Ephesus (2:1-7), establishes many of the marks of Christian authenticity, repeated in a number of the following letters as well. In verses 2-3, 'patient endurance' is mentioned twice, connected with 'bearing up' and not growing weary 'for my name's sake', which is presumably a reference to the burdens carried for being a Christian. What the Ephesian Christians will not bear (same verb), however, is the evil of false teachers, pseudo apostles, whom they have tested and find to be liars. All this is perhaps what is meant by 'your works, your toil and your patient endurance'. Loyalty to Christ has produced a hatred of heretical teaching and behaviour, characterised as the Nicolaitans in verse 6, who are also identified in 2:14-15 with Balaam and Balak, who caused Israel to stumble into idolatry and sexual immorality. This faithful loyalty produced 'tribulation' (or affliction) and 'poverty' for the church in Smyrna also, as well as slanderous attacks from the 'synagogue of Satan' (2:9). Similarly, the church in Pergamum is commended because 'you hold fast my name and you did not deny my faith' (2:13), even though one of their number had become a martyr. The qualities praised in Thyatira perhaps summarise best the major qualities which the Lord looks for in His people. 'I know your works, your love and faith and service and patient endurance' (2:19).

They are all key New Testament qualities, frequently referenced throughout the epistles. They speak of a constant commitment to Christ, to His person and work, expressed in belief and behaviour or life-style, first against every sort of opposition and distortion. This is the mature adulthood of Ephesians 4:13-14, 'no longer ... tossed to and fro by the waves and carried about by every wind of doctrine, by human cunning, by craftiness in deceitful schemes'. Even a church like Philadelphia, which had 'but little power', has nevertheless 'kept my word about patient endurance and not denied my name', to earn the Lord's commendation (3:8-10).

All these qualities are set within a context of conflict, against the background of unbelieving hostility, both religious and secular. They remind us that one of the greatest necessities of faithful ministry is to see produced Christian believers who, in Paul's framework of reference, 'take up the whole armour of God' so that they will be 'able to withstand in the evil day, and having done all, to stand firm' (Eph. 6:13). That is why the exposition and application of Scripture is so essential for the well-being of every local congregation. There is an all too real spiritual battle constantly raging, in which every believer is involved. This is not against flesh and blood, 'but against the rulers, against the authorities, against the cosmic powers over this present darkness, against the spiritual forces of evil in the heavenly places' (Eph. 6:12). It would be the height of folly, virtually spiritual suicide, not to be fully armed and alert, with 'the sword of the Spirit, which is the word of God' (Eph. 6:17).

This explains why each of the letters to the churches in Revelation ends with the words of the Lord Jesus, 'To the one who conquers'. This is elaborated once, in the letter to Thyatira, with the addition 'who keeps my works until the end' (2:26). And it is the perspective of the end, the fulfilment of all things in the eternal kingdom, which is both the motivation and reward of the faithful believer. Just to list the blessings which Christ promises to His faithful people provides the greatest of incentives to keep firm in the faith. To eat of the tree of life in the paradise of God (2:7), to not be hurt by the second death (2:11), to receive the hidden manna and a new name (2:17), to be given authority over the nations and the morning star (2:26-28), the pledge of a new eternal day, to be clothed in white garments and to have one's name written indelibly in the book of life (3:5), to be a pillar in God's temple, marked with God's name (3:12), to sit with the Lord on His throne (3:21). 'Be faithful unto death and I will give you the crown of life' (2:10).

The eternal perspective governing our present experience is one of the most important motivators in our pursuit of Christian maturity, both for ourselves and our hearers. And yet how often it is under-stated or even ignored. Part of this is a sort of embarrassment which has developed by being over-sensitive to the mockery and criticism of the unbelieving world. 'Pie-in-the-sky when you die' is used typically to dismiss the life of the world to come as an unsubstantiated fantasy. But it can cut deep and we can find ourselves consequently toning down the glorious certainties of the Scriptures about the eternal realities. If that becomes true of what we customarily call heaven, how much more today will the totally unacceptable teaching about hell be played down, or omitted? Compulsory heaven for all has become the mantra for those in our culture who still believe in life after death. People are constantly encouraged to think that someone who has died is 'looking down on us' benignly, still entering in to our everyday lives, which is the real fantasy. But there is also embarrassment that the life of the world to come can sound like a carrot to bribe us to surrender our autonomy for an uncertain paradise beyond the grave.

The gospel of grace soon undermines that form of works religion, when we realise that gratitude and godliness are the product of receiving God's mercy, not the payment required. But we need genuinely to ask ourselves whether our preaching truly reflects the huge emphasis which the Bible puts on the future kingdom, as the great unseen reality. Or have we become so distracted by both the blessings and challenges of life in this present world, that we have all but forgotten that 'faith is the assurance of things hoped for, the conviction of things not seen' (Heb. 11:1)?

Ironically, the more our teaching and preaching concentrates on knowing the blessings of God in the present world, the 'now' blessings we might well call them, the less appetite we shall have for the 'not yet' and the less equipped we shall be to stand firm in the faith. We see this in its extreme form in the various versions of the so-called 'prosperity gospel', which is certainly not good news and which seems only to make its preachers prosperous. At root, it promises all the imaginable blessings of the new creation to be available here and now, if only one has enough faith. So faith becomes a self-generated 'work', which has to be worked up in order to work out. You put in the 'faith' and God will provide the blessing. But while we may dismiss this in its crudest forms, it is very possible for us to be conditioned by a more sophisticated, 'spiritual' version of the same. It happens when our focus moves from 'what no eye has seen, nor ear heard, nor the heart of man imagined, what God has prepared for those who love him' (1 Cor. 2:9) to a this-world focus and a need-centred approach to the life of faith. If the emphasis is on God as the one who meets our felt needs, the focus will inevitably shift from Him to us. I shall begin to think that perhaps the world does revolve around me rather than being God-centred.

Our needs, however, will be as numerous as the multiple voices of our secular environment. All day long we are being told what we need to make us the self we want to be. Advertising, the media, social interaction – they all bombard us with visual and aural stimuli to tell us what we need to be complete, to protect us, fulfil us, give security, peace of mind and so on. When we are conscious that our needs are unmet, as Christians we instinctively turn to God. But we start then to regard God as a 'God of the gaps', which in this case are our unmet needs. There is a tyranny here. When our needs dominate, they become our idols, in the sense that we work and spare no effort to gratify them, whether religiously or not. And because they are so many and so demanding, we find ourselves imprisoned by them, deprived of our spiritual freedom and fulfilment in knowing the true God. Of course, Paul was right that God 'will supply every need of yours according to his riches in glory in Christ Jesus' (Phil. 4:19) but that is where our focus needs to be, on Christ's eternal glory, not on our needs. That will transform our whole perspective of the here and now.

However, there is another equally important strand of instruction we need to glean from the letters to the churches in Revelation, which concerns the negatives which the Lord identifies and rebukes in these congregations. Broadly, they comprise two main categories, which we might summarise as doctrinal and experiential. It seems that none of the churches has yet succumbed to the false teaching and distortions, but in Pergamum and Thyatira there are the warning signs that they are already present in the congregations (2:14-15) and far from being exposed and rejected they are being tolerated. 'But I have this against you, that you tolerate that woman Jezebel, who calls herself a prophetess and is teaching and seducing my servants to practice sexual immorality and to eat food sacrificed to idols' (2:20).

The progression is very significant. It begins with false 'prophecy' from a self-appointed messenger, whose false teaching seduces those who accept it into ungodly life-styles, characterised by idolatry and immorality. The two always go hand in hand in Scripture and in life. The battle is always in and for the mind. When once the thinking moves from the truth, the pattern of life will soon be defiled. From this we can deduce that the apostolic ministry not only taught the truth positively, but exposed and undermined the distortions, and we must do the same. Often the most effective way to teach the truth is to expose the counterfeit errors which are seeking to modify and eventually replace it. Indeed, it is evident that you cannot teach the positives adequately unless you deal with the negatives that oppose and deny them.

The other major thread, however, concerns the inner spiritual life and state of the churches. Ephesus has 'abandoned the love you had at first' (2:4). Sardis is warned,

'You have the reputation of being alive, but you are dead. Wake up and strengthen what remains and is about to die, for I have not found your works complete in the sight of my God' (3:1-2). Laodicea is neither hot nor cold. 'So because you are lukewarm...I will spit you out of my mouth. For you say, I am rich, I have prospered, and I need nothing, not realizing that you are wretched, pitiable, poor, blind and naked' (3:16-17). The common thread seems to be that each of these churches is unaware of their true condition and their precarious position. Love for Christ, zeal in His service and humble dependence on His grace are all conditions of heart from which both individuals and congregations can move imperceptibly, without even being aware of it. Love becomes duty; zeal is reduced to maintenance mode; humble dependence is eclipsed by pride of achievement and self-reliance.

Clearly, these are deficiencies which are highly likely to affect any of us personally, or the congregations we are called to serve. We need to be vigilant about these dangers (and others like them) which are pernicious because they drain the life from the body, but are often invisible and so unperceived. However, the answer is not for the pastor-teacher to build his ministry around a constant focus on all the deficiencies, real and imaginary, of himself and his people. Such negativity is only likely to deepen the problems. There are congregations which are made to feel that they can never get anything right, because the pastor is always after them with his big stick to make them better Christians.

But such a methodology is ineffective theologically, because it is the grace of God in the gospel of Christ that transforms the inner life and not the application of human rules and regulations, however sincere the pastor may seem to be. It is also ineffective relationally because God's sheep are to be fed and led, not driven. There may well be something fairly deep and hidden in the preacher's heart, which may need to be identified here. With the help of the Lord we need honestly to ask ourselves what is motivating our ministry. As soon as it becomes about numbers, having more members than the church down the street, planting more new congregations, being more successful in ministry than my competitors, it will inevitably grow more self-centred and self-promotional. Such a pastor is riding the proverbial tiger and it does not have a happy ending. We do well to heed John the Baptist's words, 'He must increase, but I must decrease' (John 3:30).

Unless we settle these issues (and we shall need to do this multiple times) we shall become driven preachers and driven preachers try to drive others, to make them in their own image. So they begin to pontificate, to increase the volume and intensity and reduce the relational content. But when I am sitting in the congregation, I don't want to be spoken down to, from a height, at volume. I don't want to be treated condescendingly, as though I have to be brought under the preacher's control, to fulfil his prized agenda. I want to be encouraged to be under God's authority, mediated through His Word and by His Spirit and that is not at all the same as the preacher imposing his priorities and seeking to run my life. There needs to be an element of conversation and relational warmth in the preacher's content and manner. He needs to come down from his high horse, to be less declamatory and more persuasive. I want to be spoken to as a fellow human-being, a fellow sinner, a fellow struggler, a fellow disciple. I want to be reasoned with and persuaded of the truth, because confidence in preaching is not at all the same thing as dominance.

So, when we come to examine the master's methods back in Revelation, they are strikingly straightforward and uncomplicated. The remedies for all the deficiencies are contained in the imperatives. For Ephesus, 'Remember therefore from where you have fallen; repent, and do the works you did at first' (2:5). For Smyrna, 'Do not fear … Be faithful unto death' (2:10). For Pergamum, 'Repent' (2:16). For Thyatira, 'Hold fast what you have until I come' (2:25). For Sardis, 'Wake up, and strengthen what remains … Remember, then, what you received and heard. Keep it and repent' (3:2-3). For Philadelphia, 'Hold fast what you have, so that no one may seize your crown' (3:11). For Laodicea, 'I counsel you to buy from me … so be zealous and repent' (3:18-19). What are we teaching our congregations about the normal Christian life? Do they know that it is joyful and fulfilling, but not triumphalist; hard-working and zealous, but not self-confident; every day at the cross in renewed repentance and the deepening dependence of Christ-centred faith? These are the long-term values that shape individuals and churches, down the decades and 'through all the changing scenes of life.'

7.

Preaching: Colossians
a test case

In studying the letters to the seven churches in Revelation, it was striking to realise what a mixed bag those congregations were. Some were remaining faithful to Christ and the gospel, while others were in danger of abandoning the truth, as some of their members were already falling under the spell of false teachers. Yet in chapter 1 they are represented as seven gold lampstands and in their midst the risen, glorified Lord stands (Rev. 1:12-13). Moreover, their 'angels' (most probably meaning messengers or pastors) are held, as seven stars, in the Lord's right hand (Rev. 1:16, 20). He cares for them deeply, in spite of, and perhaps because of, their imperfections. He longs for them to be overcomers, to stand firm in their faith and to experience increasingly in time, and then in eternity, all the blessings that are implicit in the gospel. Surely, that is what every faithful pastor-teacher desires for the flock for which he has responsibility. However, if these congregations, with such direct access to apostolic teaching, were so unstable and so easily diverted, we would be naïve in the extreme if we were not to realise that, two thousand years later, the problems are likely to have multiplied considerably.

'Not that I have already obtained … or am already perfect, but I press on …' (Phil. 3:12). What Paul was highlighting from his own experience is certainly echoed in every individual Christian's life and must therefore be true of every local church. The perfectibility of the church in this world is a vain quest that will always end in disappointment. Whether in the first or the twenty-first century, or anywhere in between, the constants remain the same. The gospel remains the same as 'the faith that was once for all delivered to the saints' (Jude 3), because, 'Jesus Christ is the same yesterday and today and forever' (Heb. 13:8). Human nature remains the same, since 'all have sinned and (continue to) fall short of the glory of God' (Rom. 3:23). The fallen world remains fallen and lost in its rebellion against the Creator, 'following the prince of the power of the air, the spirit that is now at work in the sons of disobedience' (Eph. 2:2), because 'the whole world lies in the power of the evil one' (1 John 5:19). But far from this providing reasons to accept the status quo and to ease off the accelerator, in New Testament thinking this is the motivation to 'press on'. Indeed, it explains why so much of the teaching of Scripture is geared not simply to the correction of erroneous thinking and sinful behaviour, but to the promotion of spiritual well-being, healthy growth and developing godliness among believers. Jesus' promise to build His church (Matt. 16:18) is not only a reference to quantity but also to quality as the people of God experience progressive deliverance from the devil and all his works.

It is instructive, therefore, to look back to the major tactics and content of the apostolic methodology, as they sought to work, as Christ's messengers, towards achieving their master's purpose for His body, the church, of which He is the head (Eph. 4:15). 'Christ loved the church and gave himself up for her … so that he might present the church to himself in splendour, without spot or wrinkle or any such thing, that she might be holy and without blemish' (Eph. 5:25, 27). In later chapters, we shall look at a number of passages in more detail, in which specific issues, dangers and problems are addressed, but first there is real value in taking one unit of Scripture and treating it as an entity in order to discover how an inspired apostle deals with a typical set of problems and needs. For greater ease in doing this, while it would be a useful approach to any letter of the New Testament, I have chosen to work with a reasonably short epistle, so that we can try to grasp more fully how the whole unit is constructed to produce Christ-like maturity. Our test case is the letter to the Colossians, a church Paul did not plant, with a membership he did not know and which may therefore have a more obvious general application to us centuries later.

Colossae was situated in Asia Minor, about a hundred miles east of Ephesus, in the Lycus Valley, near to Laodicea and Hierapolis, which are also mentioned in the letter (4:13). The church was apparently founded through the gospel ministry of Epaphras (1:7), who was a Colossian (4:12) as was Onesimus (4:9). This plant probably first took root during the time when Paul was for three years in Ephesus (Acts 20:31) and 'all the residents of Asia heard the word of the Lord, both Jews and Greeks' (Acts 19:10).

Now, around A.D. 60-62, Paul is imprisoned in Rome (Acts 28:30-31) from where he writes his letters to Ephesus, Philemon and Colossae. Epaphras is with Paul in Rome, bringing a good report from Colossae of their 'love in the Spirit' (1:8) but also doubtless news of the many problems and confusion in which the church is embroiled and which move Paul to write.

The progression of the letter is straightforward enough. After the usual formal introduction (1:1-2) Paul expresses his thanks to God for the marks of authenticity and reality in the church, which are evidence of the fruit of the true gospel of God's grace at work in their lives (1:3-8). This is followed by his prayer that they will be filled with the knowledge of God's will and strengthened with the power of God's might (1:9-14). A key teaching section follows (one of the clearest Christological passages in the whole of the New Testament) in which Christ is proclaimed as creator and controller of the cosmos and of the church (1:15-20), reminding the readers that His reconciling work is to present them 'holy and blameless and above reproach before him' (1:21-23). From here, Paul expounds on his own ministry, its goals and purpose, its contents and cost, with special regard to the benefits that it provides for the church (1:24-2:5). The opening section climaxes with an exhortation statement, which several commentators have identified as the key to the letter, 'Therefore, as you received Christ Jesus the Lord, so walk in him, rooted and built up in him and established in the faith, just as you were taught, abounding in thanksgiving' (2:6-7).

From this foundation, Paul begins his polemic against the false teaching and erroneous influences which are diverting the church. These he identifies as human tradition, legalism, mysticism and ascetic practices (2:8-23), all of which stand in opposition and as empty alternatives to the fulness of life in Christ. The transforming power of Christ is then expounded (3:1-4) with its outworking in what is to be 'put to death' (3:5-11) and what is to be 'put on' instead (3:12-17). The further practical application of this teaching is then made to family life and work situations (3:18 – 4:1). The final instructions focus on private prayer (4:2-4) and public witness (4:5-6), before the letter concludes with an extensive range of personal news and greetings (4:7-18).

This is the way the letter proceeds, with the logical development of its argument and exhortations and it would of course be entirely appropriate to teach it consecutively, section by section: dealing with the exegesis and explanation of the text. But if that is the preacher's sole approach there is a real danger that the material will be de-contextualized, that it may become overly generalised and so lose the cutting-edge which it was designed to have for its original recipients. If we are going to be teaching for maturity the expositor will need to dig deeper, or to approach the material from other angles, to get beneath the surface. We shall need to move from the plain meaning to the particular significance, if we are to connect with the original purpose of the letter's inspiration and its preservation for the church, over the last two millennia. This is largely achieved by asking the question 'Why?', beginning with the discovery of what the situation was in Colossae which Paul addresses.

The majority of the church seem to have been Gentile converts and Paul several times reminds them of just what their condition was when Christ met with them. They were 'alienated and hostile in mind, doing evil deeds' (1:21), 'dead in your trespasses and the uncircumcision of your flesh' (2:13), their lives characterised by 'what is earthly in you: sexual immorality, impurity, passion, evil desire and covetousness, which is idolatry' (3:5). The transformation that the gospel has brought is both dynamic and radical in its effects and that centres entirely on Christ Jesus the Lord.

On this basis, Paul next alerts them to the perilous dangers with which they are toying. The positive exhortations show up and highlight the opposite patterns which the Colossians are in danger of adopting, or drifting into. They must 'continue in the faith, stable and steadfast, not shifting from the hope of the gospel' (1:23). The danger is that they will move away from gospel foundations. They are to walk in Christ and be 'built up in him and established in the faith' (2:6-7). The danger is that they will live by other values, that the way 'on' for them and their Christian experience will be fatally different from their way 'in', that they will be taken captive by 'empty deceit' (2:8). They are to put to death what is earthly, to put away all the evidences of the old sinful life (3:5-11). The danger is that they will forget that 'on account of these the wrath of God is coming' (3:6) and that God's purpose for them is to be 'being renewed in knowledge after the image of its creator' (3:10).

However, Paul ramps up the magnification level, by focusing on the specifics of where they were going wrong and the false steps they were taking. There has been a great deal of scholarly speculation about the details beyond those which are stated in the text, but our task is to stay on the line of Scripture and not to be side-tracked by the curiosity of conjecture. That could prove to be very Colossian! Their primary mistake was to rely on human thinking, rather than divine revelation. 'See to it that no one takes you captive by philosophy and empty deceit, according to human tradition, according to the elemental spirits (or "principles" ESV footnote) of the world, and not according to Christ' (2:8). The four elements of the first part of the verse are each one antithetical to the last five words of the verse. They are 'not according to Christ'. There is a stark choice here between what is human, what is of the world and what is of Christ. The implication is clearly that you cannot have both. There is no 'foot in both camps' mentality possible in Christian discipleship. To rely on human tradition is to put your confidence in what is transient ('All flesh is as grass') and what will ultimately prove to be empty and deceitful in comparison to the fulness that is in Christ. 'For in him the whole fulness of deity dwells bodily', as the very next verse states unequivocally (2:9). It is a choice between time and eternity, because 'the world is passing away along with its desires, but whoever does the will of God abides forever' (1 John 2:17).

There is clearly an important lesson here for the pastor-teacher. Maturity will only be advanced when a believer recognises the radical change of life-source, and therefore life-style, which conversion brings. A preaching theme in Colossians is that all God's fulness resides in Christ, so that there cannot be any possible experience of fulness beyond the indwelling life of Christ within the believer. 'You have been filled in him, who is the head of all rule and authority' (2:10). To look elsewhere for fulfilment is crazy, especially when the object is 'the elemental principles of the world'. The root idea is to be marching in the ranks of those whose guiding principles are entirely of this world, but they must not be regarded as merely a neutral, or even harmless, alternative. They are seeking to 'take captive' the unwary believer. 'In Col 2:8 the verb is used figuratively of drawing someone away from the truth of Christ into the slavery of error. Paul warns the converts at Colossae against the threat of being seduced from the Lord. His verb gives the picture of prisoners being led away with a rope around their necks, like the long strings of captives portrayed on Assyrian monuments.'[1] We may well need to use more of such vivid imagery to bring home to our generation the dangers of compromise with the world's thinking and behaviour. Don't become a prisoner of war! It can all look so seductively attractive until the trap is sprung; but it is the mark of Christian maturity to detect the deceit inherent in the desires of the flesh and the desires of the eyes and the pride of life. What is promised is never delivered.

However, it is instructive that the same word (stoicheia) translated 'elemental principles' in 2:8 recurs in 2:20, where it is associated with the rules and regulations of asceticism. Snares to true Christian discipleship can lurk in religiosity, as much as in secular thinking. H. H. Esser helpfully comments, 'They, "the elements of the world", cover all the things in which man places his trust apart from the living God revealed in Christ; they become his gods, he

1. N. Hillyer in 'The New International Dictionary of New Testament Theology,' Vol. 3; Exeter, Paternoster, 1978; p. 379.

becomes their slave.'[2] In context, the slavery concerned is identified as submission to dogmatic instructions, 'Do not handle. Do not taste. Do not touch' (2:21), which Paul identifies as 'according to human precepts and teachings' (2:22). The motivation or attraction of such rules is to stop the indulgence of the flesh. Indeed, as he admits, they have 'an appearance of wisdom', but this is the empty deceit of the 'stoicheia'. For generations ascetic practices have been advocated as a means of mortifying the flesh, all the way from Simon Stylites, who lived for thirty-six years in great austerity at the top of a pillar, essentially sixty feet up, to the giving up of chocolate for Lent, by well-heeled western church-goers. But Paul's indictment is that 'they are of no value' (2:23). You do not become holy by what you give up. That is 'self-made religion' (2:23).

Earlier in the chapter, Paul has also identified two other siren calls which can lure the believer away from the fulness of life in Christ and which is in Him alone. 2:16 refers to questions of food and drink, festivals, new moons and Sabbath days. Such legalism, like the ascetic practices mentioned above, does not open up the way to godliness. The Old Testament regulations were only 'a shadow of the things to come, but the substance belongs to Christ' (2:17). Once again we are reminded that what is being looked for is to be found in its entirety in Christ. Similarly, mysticism with its emphasis on super-spiritual experiences, such as visions, or the worship of angels can only rob the believer of all that should be theirs in Christ (2:18). Again, Paul pulls no punches in his directness about such disastrous

---

2. H. H. Esser, ibid., Vol. 2; p. 453.

diversions. That route involves being 'puffed up without reason by his sensuous mind', which inevitably means 'not holding fast to the Head' (2:18b-19).

For the Bible teacher, however, not only the identification of these prevalent dangers but also the spiritual reasoning as to why they are to be rejected is very significant. Error falls when the truth is stated and expounded and that truth is 'Christ in you, the hope of glory' (1:28), or, as the next chapter affirms, 'You have died and your life is hidden with Christ in God' (3:3). In 2:11-15, Paul expounds the essential unity which believers have with Christ. The putting off of the flesh, the old pre-Christian way of life, occurs at the moment of the new birth and is therefore totally dependent on Christ's death and resurrection, which is a finished work with eternal consequences. Reconciled to God in Christ's body of flesh by His death (1:22), all that circumcision and the other Old Testament rites and ceremonies pre-figured has been fulfilled in Christ (2:11). Through His death on the cross, 'the record of debt that stood against us with its legal demands' has been cancelled and set aside (2:14). Moreover, having been forgiven all our trespasses, God made us alive together with the risen Christ, so that we share in His victory over all the hostile powers (2:13-15). That is why the empty promises of the 'stoicheia' are totally irrelevant for the person who is in Christ. They can offer nothing alongside 'the riches of full assurance of understanding and the knowledge of God's mystery, which is Christ, in whom are hidden all the treasures of wisdom and knowledge' (2:2-3).

So this now explains why Paul defines his own apostolic ministry as a stewardship given to him from

God, 'to make the word of God fully known' and to proclaim 'the riches of the glory of this mystery, which is Christ in you, the hope of glory'. It teaches us why he affirms so strongly, '<u>Him</u> we proclaim ... that we may present everyone mature in Christ' (1:25-28). This is God's divinely-given route to Christian maturity and there is no alternative way! This is confirmed, throughout the letter, by Paul's persistence in establishing the person and work of Christ as the central reality of true Christian experience, because it is the foundational demonstration of God's intervening grace in the gospel. The remedy for all the Colossian ills lies in the rediscovery of the total sufficiency and indispensable centrality of Christ Jesus the Lord, in both the objective content of the good news ('the riches of the glory of this mystery' 1:27) and its subjective experience. 'For in him the whole fulness of deity dwells bodily, and you have been filled in him, who is the head of all rule and authority' (2:9-10). The release for those who have been taken captive and the preventative action for those unaffected as yet are both the same; to proclaim Christ (1:28). And the whole letter illustrates the depths and riches of what that means.

It is often said that pastors should preach the gospel in every sermon, because all of life's problems ultimately find their resolution in Christ and His cross. That is undoubtedly true, but it has sadly often degenerated into a 'simple gospel' approach which deprives the hearers of the depths, breadth and scope contained in the Biblical exposition of the gospel. Every sermon should honour and exalt Christ, as all the Scriptures bear witness to Him, but just to recognise that reality should lead us to emulate Paul's humility, awe and reverence before the divine revelation. 'Oh, the depth of the riches and wisdom and knowledge of God! How unsearchable are his judgments and how inscrutable his ways!' (Rom. 11:33). The Colossians had certainly come to a saving knowledge of the truth, but if that was to root and grow, it had to become much more substantial, which is why the letter is such a rich source for our own deeper understanding of the Christ whom we proclaim. This is not the place for a detailed exposition of the letter, but even a brief survey of Paul's approach indicates his confidence that teaching the fulness of Christ is the key to keeping the church on the track.

The prayer (1:9-12), which introduces the main body of the letter's teaching, combines the twin goals to which the Colossians were aspiring – knowledge and experience, as Paul is asking God to fill them 'with the knowledge of his will in all spiritual wisdom and understanding', because that will issue in a life 'fully pleasing to him, bearing fruit in every good work'. This will require nothing less than God's power if they are to persevere with joy and thankfulness. It is important, therefore, that the dimensions of that 'glorious might' should be understood by his readers, which leads Paul to his eulogy concerning Christ in 1:15-20. This magnificent statement is effectively a series of credal affirmations about who Christ is and how His power is exercised. In His relationship to God, the Father (cf 1:3), He is the 'eikon', the image, or exact representation of the invisible God in human form. In relation to the created order, He is the 'firstborn', which means that He preceded the whole creation and that He is its sovereign ruler. Verses 16-17 stress the totality of

His supremacy by the repeated use of 'all things'. Nothing is excluded, as verse 16 affirms 'in heaven and on earth, visible and invisible'. Nothing exists apart from His creative will and everything is 'held together' in Him, as John 1:3 and Hebrews 1:2 also confirm.

At this point we begin to see how angled the teaching is to the Colossian issues. How can there be anything or anyone superior to Christ? They are all under His dominion. Verse 18 then transfers this revelation of the Lord of the universe to the church, the body of which He is the head. Just as He is the sovereign over the creation, as the 'firstborn', so He is the firstborn from the dead, the creator and head of the new order, His born again people. Whether in the old order or the new His supremacy is total (v. 18), which leads to the climax of the description in verse 19, that 'in him all the fulness of God was pleased to dwell'. And yet that magnificent declaration of the glories of Christ is immediately related to the locus where it is most perfectly displayed, 'making peace by the blood of his cross' (v. 20). The truth of who Christ is and what He has accomplished demolishes the foolish delusions of Paul's readers that there might be some 'fulness' to be found outside of, or beyond, Christ Jesus, the Lord.

The rest of the teaching section explains and explores the implications of this central foundation in a number of ways. He is able to make His people 'holy and blameless' (1:21-23). His presence in the Christian's life now is the guarantee of future glory and the path to developing maturity (1:24-29). A full understanding of 'God's mystery, which is Christ' unites and encourages the church, and preserves believers from the delusion of 'plausible arguments' (2:1-5). The corrective passages we have already examined then follow (2:6-23), leading to the climax of 3:1-4. Here the union of the Christian believer 'with Christ' in being raised to newness of life and having died to the old sinful way of life, is taught both as doctrinal reality and personal spiritual motivation. The Christ who died, was raised and is seated at the right hand of the Father is the one about whom Paul can say 'he is your life' and 'you will appear with him in glory' (3:4). So, 'Set your minds on things that are above, not on things that are on earth' (3:2), such as the plausible arguments and empty deceit of the 'stoicheia'.

The clear teaching content of the letter is that God's fulness is to be found in Jesus Christ alone. Nothing can be added to the full sufficiency of the life of God, planted in the soul of every believer 'in Christ'. To look for a gospel which is 'Jesus plus' is actually to consign oneself to a message of 'Jesus minus'. As soon as we think anything can be added to Him and all that we have in Him, we demean His glory and imply that He is not enough. In fact we reduce His supremacy to dimensions of our own choosing and exalt ourselves above God Himself, 'for in Christ all the fulness of God was pleased to dwell' (1:19).

Colossians provides us with a representative example of the sort of teaching that is needed to keep our hearers firmly on the line of God's unchanging truth. Because its content is so central to the whole Biblical revelation of salvation, it also reminds us that we need to be teaching our hearers not only the truth but that it is the truth. There is a real and present danger that in a cultural context where the existence of any absolute truth is denied, a distinctively

Christian mind-set, which not only receives God's truth but is consistently shaped by it, becomes increasingly rare. The prevailing attitude of our hearers may well be that the Bible has some interesting ideas and contains some helpful directions, but that its message can be assessed and sieved, according to the appeal that it makes to us today. Much as the preaching performance is silently judged by how it 'comes across', so the message itself can be the casualty of the same process of me-centred discrimination. Then the questions are no longer, 'Is it true? Does it work?' but rather 'Do I like it? Am I comfortable with it?' The answer, however, is not to quit the field, but to resolve to preach the truth in an uncompromising but convincing way, as the great realities of the faith are declared and explained, from the Bible's own context, in the Bible's own words. How to develop such a Christian mind-set in the hostile contemporary context is what must concern us next.

8.

Preaching to renew minds

John Stott once famously described the purpose of preaching as being two-fold: to disturb the comfortable and to comfort the disturbed. Today we are very happy with the ministry of 'comfort' in most of our congregations, but much more resistant to whatever might disturb. Of course Stott's point was that the disturbance is essential before the comfort can be prescribed. Not only is that hard to take, but we also like to redefine 'comfort' along the lines of cups of hot chocolate on cold winter evenings, or chicken soup, or whatever will make us feel better. However, when God called Isaiah to 'comfort' His people with the promise of the ending of the exile and the restoration that would follow (Isa. 40:1ff) the verb had a different connotation, perhaps more akin to our modern 'Take heart!' God's comfort breathes new life into His demoralised, defeated people. It strengthens and enables, so that they can deal with their fears and move forward in faith.

Yet this sort of bracing encounter is not what the average congregation is expecting on a Sunday morning. In many church contexts we seem to have succumbed to a silent conspiracy not to rock the boat, in which both preacher and congregation have become complicit. Biblical truth is to be taught, but it needs to be made as safe as possible. The text is utilised to reinforce a few basic Christian principles, on which we all broadly agree, but not to challenge at the deeper levels of our ongoing personal difficulties, battles and anxieties and certainly not to address the social, political or cultural issues with which the rest of the world is obsessed twenty-four/seven. Sunday church becomes a cosy 'bubble', a retreat which refreshes and reinforces us to get through another week, but fundamentally nothing changes. In pursuit of 'comfort' and reassurance the text is effectively domesticated simply by being de-contextualised. The objective content of its truth is sacrificed on the altar of our 'feel good' demands. The text serves to provide a moral lesson, or a general spiritual 'thought', well supported by emotional or amusing illustrations, which may well produce a satisfied, but fundamentally complacent and unchanged, group of hearers. Preaching like this (and sadly it seems common) does not transform the church and so will certainly then never change the world.

There is an interesting paradox at work here. On the one hand our contemporary culture values personal freedom to live my life my way as the greatest good, providing only that I do not harm others. For many people the stress of daily life prompts an almost endless quest for 'peace and quiet', the avoidance of hassle, minimal disagreement and controversy. On the other hand, the media, both social and public, constantly provoke and promote controversy and antagonism, in every area of life. This is often pursued relentlessly, sometimes even viciously, whether in personal relationships or public affairs. It is hardly surprising, therefore, that Christian people want to demonstrate the more excellent way of love and compassion as a distinctive salt and light witness in a decaying culture. The danger, however, is that this affects our Christian corporate culture as a dislike of, and recoil from, anything that could be considered 'controversial'. This mind-set will condemn our preaching to be anodyne, in that its greatest value will be seen to be the soothing application of spiritual pain-killers. However, John Stott's book title, 'Christ the controversialist', is an accurate, if compressed, summary of the ministry of Jesus.

Far from controversy being wrong in itself, however, it can in fact be very positive and beneficial. Often we only see different facets of truth when we are forced to examine opposite or antagonistic views of a particular issue. But everything depends on how the controversy is conducted and this, in turn, will hinge on the motivation behind it. Not every battle Christians become involved in is necessarily the Lord's battle. Confrontation certainly has a major role in our Christian communication, but there are equivalent temptations for the preacher at this opposite end of the 'comfort spectrum'. What am I seeking to do? Why am I introducing this controversy and for whose honour? Paul reminded the Corinthians 'we are not waging war according to the flesh' (2 Cor. 10:3).

The content of the controversy and its challenges must flow from the content of the Bible's teaching, as it impacts life in this fallen world, and not from the contentiousness of the preacher. The pulpit is not a context whose occupant can be seeking to dominate and control the lives of the hearers. To proclaim the essential truth of God-centredness involves exposing the me-centredness into which we all so readily slip, by nature. But that requires a humble servant, who is seeking honestly and uncompromisingly to deal with his own despotic ego. 'For what we proclaim is not ourselves, but Jesus Christ as Lord, with ourselves as your servants for Jesus' sake' (2 Cor. 4:5). Interestingly, even the business world identifies that the ingredients detected in 'successful' leadership include not only an intense professional commitment and determination, but also a personal humility and lack of self-absorption. Failure is apparently often attributable to the size of the leader's personal ego. 'He who has ears to hear ...!'

It was my privilege as a theological student, nearly fifty years ago, to sit at the feet of Dr J. I. Packer, whose lecture notes I have returned to, with immense profit, again and again, throughout my ministry. I do not know if he ever wrote up what follows elsewhere; at least I have not come across it if he did. But from my notes in the early '70's, on the nature of ministry, I recall that Dr Packer identified four weaknesses in both the personal and corporate spiritual cultures exemplified among evangelical Christians, which he traced back through post-Reformation history and highlighted in the later 20th century. It seems to me that not only are they still with us, but that they are even more dangerously acute today, in that they go largely unnoticed, having become accepted as normality. They provide us with a check-list of some of the areas, at least, in which a ministry of change is greatly needed in our own times.

The first characteristic cited is isolationism. This is not so much the proper response to the exhortation, 'Do not

love the world or the things in the world' (1 John 2:15),
which rightly recognises the requirement of a distinctive,
positive holiness at the heart of true discipleship. Rather,
this response is one of conscious withdrawal from the
contemporary culture into a self-sufficient, hermetically-
sealed 'bubble' of Christian fellowship, which has
minimal engagement or interaction with life outside
itself. Withdrawal can often appear to be the best godly
option when we feel overwhelmed by the many and varied
questions, challenges and sometimes dismissals, which
the unbelieving world insistently poses. Many Christians
feel themselves to be ill equipped to discover any viable
answers, let alone present them. The tendency then is to
take refuge in an anti-intellectualism, which pulls out of
the debates and contents itself instead with a preoccupation
with the orthodox doctrines we already know and hold
dear. This way means that we have no audible voice in the
public forum.

Closely related, secondly, is the danger of conformism,
which operates as a severe restraint on change, within
many Christian communities. Here the withdrawal from
the hostile world is reinforced by a code of conduct which
invests the status quo with the quality of godliness. A sort
of middle-class respectability develops, foundationally
Christian perhaps, but one in which the practical issues
have all been settled, so that what is required is adherence
to the patterns of the establishment, with little or no room
for radical questioning or re-assessment.

And the third characteristic, which is again closely
related to isolationism and conformism is legalism. This
goes beyond Scripture by making and teaching human

rules by which to govern the lives of the group members, in order to promote group solidarity and security. Though often unwritten, the rules become more and more binding. There are things 'we' (the in-group) do and other things that 'we' certainly do not! Acceptance depends on legalistic conformity and inevitably the life-style of such a group becomes increasingly tyrannical as grace is suffocated by a religion of works. Life degenerates into a stressful navigation of 'shibboleths' (see Judg. 12:5-6). This was the curse of Pharisaism, which Jesus highlighted so poignantly when He exposed their 'teaching as doctrines the commandments of men' (Matt. 15:9).

Finally, Packer identifies the problem of emotionalism, which elevates the feelings above thought and action. This may be accompanied by a good deal of excitement and even sensitivity, but in the end the stress is on what are regarded as godly 'feelings', such as joy, peace, well-being, rather than on godly action, which is the product of faith. The evidence of real faith is not to be found in the emotions, which are always transient and in flux, but in action based on God's word of promise. As James says, 'Faith by itself, if it does not have works, is dead ... Show me your faith apart from your works' (an impossibility) 'and I will show you my faith by my works' (James 2:17-18). Without such decisive action, in obedience to God's word, professed faith becomes vacillating and weak. In fact it will soon degenerate into mere sentimentality. It seems to me that this analysis is as trenchant and necessary today as ever it was. These tendencies are only too evident in our churches and which of us does not sometimes feel their strong magnetism within our own hearts?

Recognising then that confrontation and conflict are an integral ingredient of any faithful Biblical ministry, we need to turn back to the Scriptures to learn how to proceed in godly, life-transforming ways. In Corinth, Paul faced some of his toughest opponents and most testing circumstances. The indications are all there in the first letter, but it is in 2 Corinthians that this conflict occupies centre-stage as he defends his apostleship and confronts his detractors. At the start of chapter 10 there is an instructive passage which brings together Paul's personal attitude towards his readers and his methodology in the controversy. He begins, 'I, Paul, myself entreat you, by the meekness and gentleness of Christ' (v. 1). What Philip Hughes calls 'the ring of affection' is inescapable. Though he will use his apostolic authority to demolish the pretentions of the false apostles in Corinth, his motivation is not self-vindication but love for the Corinthian believers, whom he will do everything he can to rescue from the snares of heretical teachers.

The gospels are full of evidence of Christ's meek and gentle spirit, yet He also drove the money-changers from the temple and denounced the hypocrisy of the religious leaders in the most uncompromising terms. Hughes comments, 'The popular misconception that meekness and gentleness are incompatible with sternness is refuted by the example of Christ Himself' (instancing the examples quoted above). But he concludes, 'Such severity did not annul this gentleness; on the contrary, it was generated by the loving depths of His compassion for the lost'.[1] As

1. Hughes, P. E. 'Paul's Second Epistle to the Corinthians'; Eerdmans, Grand Rapids, 1962; p. 344-5.

we discuss the battles which faithful confrontational Bible
preaching may cause, we need to keep the model and
example of the Lord Jesus clearly before us and to pray
that our preaching will also be reflective of His meek and
gentle spirit.

Next, Paul explains to the Corinthians his own
convictions which shape his pastoral method. Profound
correction of un-Biblical teaching and attitudes is needed,
so he is about to engage in battle, as every faithful
pastor must. But it is not 'according to the flesh' (v. 3). In
Ephesians 6:12 he states that 'we do not wrestle against
flesh and blood'. This is not an inter-personal human
struggle, in which Paul is seeking to gain the upper hand,
or to justify himself. Nor is it a fight that can be waged with
human weapons or resources, as the following verses will
show. This is because, as he continues in Ephesians 6:12
'we wrestle against the rulers, against the authorities,
against the cosmic powers over this present darkness,
against the spiritual forces of evil in the heavenly places'.
That is why nothing less than the whole armour of God
will be adequate for the confrontation. And that is where
his confidence lies. 'For the weapons of our warfare are not
of the flesh, but have divine power to destroy strongholds.'
(2 Cor. 10:4) Only the extreme power of God is able to
pull down the devil's defences, but the agency is the human
communicator. 'We destroy arguments and every lofty
opinion raised against the knowledge of God and take
every thought captive to obey Christ' (v. 5).

These strongholds include 'arguments' (v. 5) – mind
sets, rebellious thought-patterns and the self-justification
we create for ourselves as we reject God and His Word.

They include 'lofty opinions' (v. 5), also translated 'pretensions', indicating the arrogance that claims independence of thought and action from God, that place human 'wisdom' in the place of divine revelation. They include fashionable intellectual doubts, scepticism and cynicism and the re-interpretation of the plain meaning of Scripture, which is such a convenient device, even in the church, for rationalising our refusal to bow the knee to God. These barriers to belief have to be dealt with and a teaching ministry not only seeks to do that, whenever exposition of the passage requires it, but also provides an example to our hearers of how they too can be involved in the battle.

'Taking every thought captive to obey Christ' (v. 5b) is indicative of an expedition into hostile territory, by which the truth of Scripture undermines the false thinking and brings the true freedom of submission to Christ, as Lord. When we realise the enormity of this task we can see how foolish it would be to use the world's methodology. And yet our constant temptation is to do just that. Every time we put our confidence in something other than the Word of God in the hands of the Spirit of God, to accomplish the work of God, we are returning to the flesh. The temptations are everywhere—emotional or psychological manipulation, sound-bite trivia and glib one-liners, reliance on presentation techniques, video clips, continuous appeals to self-interest, the inflation of the preacher's personality— they are all there and many more. But are we really so foolish as to put our confidence in any of these? Satan's strongholds will continue to thrive against such paper darts. Our two greatest weapons are the sword of the Spirit, the Word of

God, and prayer (Eph. 6:17-20). We have our Bibles and we
have our knees and we need to use both.[2]

One of the most important insights in these verses is
that the spiritual battle is fought in the mind, in order
to change the activity of the will. It explains why it is
important for our teaching to engage with 'the spirit of
the age', as it arrogates itself against God's revelation in
His Word, both written and incarnate. This will express
itself in different ways, at different times of history and
in different locations. It is no good re-fighting yesterday's
battles. Today we have to deal with the implausibility, in
the thinking of many, that there could ever be a divine
creator, let alone that He could decree how the life He has
given to each human being should be lived in the world
He has made. Secular humanism, post-modern nihilism,
hedonism, comparative religions – all these and many
others combine as 'every lofty opinion raised against the
knowledge of God'. But the way they will be overcome is
by the proclamation of Christ. If every thought is to be
taken captive to obey Christ, then Christ must be declared
as Saviour and Lord. Indeed, this is the 'knowledge of
God' against which the unbelieving world asserts itself.
The preaching of the whole counsel of God, in the gospel
of the person and work of Christ, is the means by which
the strongholds are demolished, but the proclamation has
to be aimed at the target. It is no good firing the guns
into the wide blue yonder. It is no good simply addressing

---

2. The substance of this material on 2 Corinthians 10:1-5 was first given in
   my address 'Preaching Truth in an Age of Idolatry,' at the International
   Congress on Preaching; Cambridge, April 2007; organised by Preaching Magazine U.S.A.; preaching.org

the Sunday morning 'bubble', as though there is no unbelieving world outside seeking to puncture and deflate it. The weapons have to be trained on to the target in the confidence that they have the divine power needed.

However, it is equally important to realise that the ultimate aim is not the destruction of the enemy, but the capture of his thinking to bring it into obedience to Christ. This happens when Christ is enthroned as Lord of the mind, as well as the heart and will, which defines the coming of the kingdom or kingly rule of God in the individual life (Luke 17:21). Of course, this is entirely the operation of God's saving grace, sovereignly raising the dead to life, according to His will. 'No one can come to me unless the Father who sent me draws him', Jesus said (John 6:44). But in that same gospel we learn that it is the lifting up of Christ, on the cross and subsequently in the preaching of Christ crucified, which 'will draw all people to myself' (John 12:32). There is no other way that anyone can come and no other message which can end the rebellion of the human heart and bring every thought into submission to Christ. But the fact that Paul is having to address Christians, who are in danger of allowing their own 'thinking' to usurp the place of Christ in their lives, indicates that this is an ongoing warfare. Believers, as much as unbelievers, are in need of this regular proclamation of Christ and the gospel, in all its fulness and in the combination of meekness and authority which characterise the Lord Himself, if they are to remain true to the faith and be effective witnesses to its power. 'The philosophies and sophistries of the 'natural' man are frequently permitted to usurp a position of influence in the redeemed intellect' (Hughes, p. 353). It is this goal of

Christian maturity to which we must both aspire and make progress, firstly for ourselves but also for all those whom we are privileged to teach. The intellectual centre of our being (what the Bible means by the heart) must be brought captive to Christ on a daily basis. It is a battle, but the divine resources are totally sufficient.

Pursuing the theme a little further in the apostolic writings will give us a firmer hold on this imperative element of developing Christian maturity, in terms of the changed mind. The general statement of Romans 12:2 positions the two alternatives in stark contrast. 'Do not be conformed to this world, but be transformed by the renewal of your mind.' The two are mutually exclusive. If the transformation is not actively happening we shall simply slip back into a 'this world' mind-set and fail to respond to the mercies of God in the gospel as we ought. It is the easiest thing in the world for the sailor to tie a loose knot around the bollards and the tide will soon do the work of drifting the boat from its moorings. But how is the mind to be renewed, for that is the means by which the whole life is to be transformed? This is what will produce in the believer a passionate commitment to the will of God as 'good and acceptable and perfect'. This idea and the same vocabulary occurs in two other important Pauline references. Col 3:10 speaks about 'the new self, which is being renewed in knowledge after the image of its creator', and this is paralleled and expanded in Ephesians 4:23-24 as 'to be renewed in the spirit of your minds, and to put on the new self, created after the likeness of God in true righteousness and holiness'. Again, the close connection of mind to godliness of behaviour is very significant.

The context of the Ephesians passage gives us considerable help. As the practical application of the epistle's magnificent teaching about Christ and the church begins at 4:17, Paul concentrates on the relationship of thought to behaviour. 'You must no longer walk as the Gentiles do, in the futility of their minds.' The idea concerns thinking that is vain or empty, that produces nothing of substance. But in the next two verses Paul explores more fully why that is so and how it has come about. This is very helpful, as it gives us insights into what will enable us to overcome the down drag of the old nature in practice. Verse 18 works to a climax of reasons as to why the non-Christian mind-set is so counter-productive, but if we read it backwards from the end it reveals the chain reaction which operates. The core problem is 'hardness of heart', which is the determined resistance to God's revelation and its application at the decision-making centre of each human personality. All that is needed for the heart to harden against God is to ignore and thereby reject His revelation, whether that is general revelation as through the creation (see Rom. 1:18-23) or the special revelation of the Scriptures of which Christ is the focus. Such hardness of heart is the cause of 'the ignorance that is in them', since rejection of God's revelatory light is to condemn oneself to the darkness of alienation from God's life and a deficient understanding of His truth. As verse 18 has delineated the inner process of rejecting God and His revelation, so verse 19 explores its ultimate outworking in behaviour, or life-style; moral numbness, overwhelming sensuality and an insatiable appetite for 'every kind of impurity'.

To alert our hearers as to how this process tightens
its grip, when once we begin to drift back towards our
old Gentile ways, is a powerful first step towards taking
action against it. Paul puts it with stark simplicity, but also
aggrieved amazement, as he bursts out, 'But that is not the
way you learned Christ' (v. 20). Nothing could be more
opposite to Christian thinking than the old unregenerate
mind-set. So, what is the route to Christian maturity
which Paul advises, which he describes as 'the truth as it
is in Jesus'? Verses 22-24 are very specific. 'To put off your
old self which belongs to your former manner of life and
is corrupt through deceitful desires' (v. 22) calls for a life
that has made a clear and decisive break, initially at the
point of the new birth, but renewed in active practice, day
by day. That is the balancing positive stress of verse 24.
'Put on the new self created after the likeness of God in
true righteousness and holiness.' The work of the gospel is
to restore progressively the image of God in the believer,
which can equally be expressed as to grow each one into
increasing likeness to the Lord Jesus. The new birth is the
critical moment at which this life begins, but just like the
putting off it is a continuing practice, which needs to be
re-affirmed and renewed daily. And that is why the key
to both of these responses is expressed in the present
continuous tense of the verb in verse 23. You were taught
'to be renewed in the spirit of your minds'.

It is easy to pass over this and not to see the enormously
helpful insights Paul is providing for his readers. His
whole emphasis is on what is going on in the mind.
The old ungodly mind-set inevitably expressed itself in
ungodly behaviour. But what brought the change about

for Paul's readers was that they 'learned Christ'. Verse 21 is significant. Paul writes, 'assuming that you have heard about him and were taught in him as the truth is in Jesus'. They heard the message and were taught its meaning and significance. They learned about the person of Christ, His nature, His work, His vindication and coming return, what we might call in shorthand terms, the gospel. However, as they recall all this, Paul's point is that the way 'on' in the Christian life, the road to maturity, depends on exactly the same principles as the way 'in'. You never stop 'learning Christ', which is why the mind must be 'being renewed' every day. That is why Paul was writing this letter and it is why the renewal of Christian minds must be a major aim of all Christian ministry. This is what will lead to real and lasting renewal and to the proper functioning of the church.

Notice that the renewal is not created by exciting, empowering experiences, by dramatic emotional crises, but by a new mind-set. Spiritual renewal is primarily about renewed thinking. The logic is obvious. We need to have minds taught by God's Spirit so that our thinking is renewed, in order to know God's will. And we need to know God's will if ever we are to live a God-pleasing life, defined for us by the example of Jesus. It was the voice of the divine Father, coming from heaven which affirmed, 'You are my beloved Son; with you I am well pleased' (Luke 3:22). He is the pattern which our renewed minds will seek to follow. So our minds will be renewed by growing in the knowledge of Christ, just as we are taught in the Scriptures. That was how we came to saving faith and that is how we will go on to maturity. Christians are renewed and become fit for purpose by hearing and learning the Word of God through expository preaching, which of course stimulates an appetite to learn more by personal acquaintance with God in our individual reading of His Word. An expository teaching ministry will produce a Bible-loving and Bible-studying congregation. That is nothing to do with verbal intelligence or academic ability and everything to do with a hunger to know God better and to develop the relationship of a dependent child upon a loving heavenly Father.

This then is the pastor's responsibility, not just from the pulpit on a Sunday (though that is paramount) but at every level throughout the whole church family. Check out what the youngest children are being taught? Is it the truth as it is in Jesus? How is the thinking of the young people being renewed through their own Bible teaching programme? What about the house groups? Have they just become chat sessions or a pooling of ignorance, or are the minds of the attenders being renewed by the living and enduring Word of God? When the Bible is being properly expounded throughout the church family, week by week, there will be an incremental growth in understanding which will develop gradually into a mature spiritual adulthood, 'to the measure of the stature of the fulness of Christ' (Eph. 4:13). Christians will have a clear head on the big issues of life. They will be evidencing good sound judgments about the decisions they have to make. They will begin to find their thinking governed by God's truth in every area of life. They will come nearer to the reality in experience of what Paul meant when he told the Corinthians, 'but we have the mind of Christ' (1 Cor. 2:16).

Before we leave this section of Scripture we need to learn from the way in which the apostle develops and applies the thesis we have been exploring. This too is instructive for us in terms of pastoral method. In verses 25-32, there are listed five examples, which each illustrate and apply the dynamic for change which he has been teaching. There is something to be put off, something to put on instead and the enabling motivation to do that is provided by the renewed mind. The first example follows the template most closely and supplies a very clear illustration of these basic pastoral principles. Verse 25 exhorts, 'Therefore, having put away falsehood, let each one of you speak the truth with his neighbour, for we are members one of another.' Put off lying. Put on truthful speech. Why? Because the renewed mind-set with its controlling focus on Christ and the gospel teaches us that we belong to one another, within the body of Christ, since each of us belongs to Him. Therefore, we shall not want to harm the body, which the gospel has created, by deceiving and misleading one another through falsehood. The remaining examples follow the same practical applicatory pattern.

Verse 26 teaches us to put off sinful anger. This is not saying that all anger is automatically sinful. There is such a thing as righteous indignation, as we see in Christ's cleansing of the temple (John 2:13-17), but most of our anger is far from righteous. It is when anger is treasured and rehearsed beyond the end of the day that it begins to fester and becomes increasingly difficult to deal with, which gives the devil 'an opportunity' within the church to sow seeds of discord and strife which are the opposite of gospel unity. The third example (v. 28) puts off stealing and puts on honest work, because the renewed gospel mind wants to 'have something to share with anyone in need'.

The target in verse 29 is 'corrupting talk' which needs to be replaced by that which is 'good for building up' and is a means of grace to those who hear it. The gospel motivation in verse 30 is that the Christian's life is sealed by the Spirit (see Eph. 1:13) as the mark of God's ownership, so do not grieve the Spirit because you are to be living now in light of the 'day of redemption'. Finally all forms of malice are to be rejected and replaced by kindness, tender-heartedness and mutual forgiveness, with the gospel mind-set motivation that 'God in Christ forgave you' (v. 31-32). It is striking how practical and comparatively detailed these examples are, but it is especially the renewed gospel mind which is at the heart of the new Christian life-style, 'the new self created after the likeness of God'.

By hearing Scripture expounded faithfully and well the hearers' minds have every opportunity to be renewed. The motivation is neither the threats implicit in legalism nor the self-indulgence of a laissez-faire version of 'discipleship'. It is the gospel of the grace of God in Christ Jesus. This emphasis will need to be represented in our preaching for maturity too, if we are to have any lasting effect for good. It will lead to greater godliness as believers discern the will of God for their daily lives and begin to live it out in all their thinking and actions. And in this way the church develops its true characteristic as the prototype in time of what God will bring about in eternity, 'to unite all things in Christ, things in heaven and things on earth' (Eph. 1:10).

9.

Preaching that is balanced and well crafted

In the first two decades of the twenty-first century books about preaching seem to have become a heavy industry. From the detailed treatments of every aspect of preaching preparation and methodology, to sceptical enquiries as to whether preaching has any future at all, in our digital age, there is no shortage of opinion and advice from across the whole theological spectrum. Much depends ultimately on the theological position and pre-suppositions of the writers, which is especially the case with regard to their beliefs concerning the authority of the Bible. Still in most churches of whatever theological hue the Bible is read during the public worship setting, even if in a very abbreviated form. Yet even in Biblically orthodox churches, what would have been regarded as the minimal norm not long ago—a Biblical 'call to worship', a congregational psalm, Old and New Testament readings—seems to have been largely eroded into one passage, from which the sermon will be preached.

However, it is precisely the preacher's attitude towards the Bible that will determine how he thinks about his preaching and will shape the foundation assumptions he will bring with him to the task. There is undoubtedly an increase in the number of local church ministers and lay preachers committed to Biblical preaching, at least theoretically, and often seeking help to do the job better. But at the same time, the multiplication of training resources and diversification of theological approaches can present a bewildering maze of both challenges and opportunities, which may induce a paralysing effect. The danger then is to opt for whichever 'method' appears most attractive, or is most readily at hand, and then for that emphasis, which may be very helpful in itself, to become the major controlling factor in one's preaching, to the exclusion of other equally significant strands. The result can be an imbalance, which, while seeking to be Biblical in one area, deprives the congregation of the whole counsel of God in others. A good and necessary emphasis can actually end up having a negative influence, if it begins to become overly dominant and exclusive.

Preaching can be compared to wood carving. The aim is to take the original natural product and with the application of creativity, knowledge and skill, to use a range of tools at the carver's disposal so as to produce an article, which is hopefully both useful and well-made. For the 'preacher-carver' the challenge is similar. The original product with which he must work is a given—not a block of divinely created wood, but a section of divinely breathed text—to which he needs to apply knowledge and skill in order to present its essential message in a form which is both faithful and beneficial. Of course, this is not a perfect analogy since the Biblical text has its own life which determines the sermon shape in a way that an inert block of wood does not. But what perhaps does resonate is that the carver has a set of tools at his disposal, to achieve certain ends, which are appropriate to different types of wood (genres of Scripture), and which, by practice and skill, enable him to release the potential of the material. What he does not do is to apply the same tool to every part of the task. There is, however, a danger that the Biblical preacher can become a one-tool practitioner using the same basic approach to every text. There are at least four examples we may observe of this commonly happening, which I hope will help to clarify the point.

The first is the mantra 'the gospel every Sunday', which promotes a commitment to preaching the gospel as the central focus and purpose of every sermon. From one perspective that concern is thoroughly Biblical. All Scriptures bear witness to Christ and He is their centre and fulfilment. 'Him we proclaim' is Paul's summary of his apostolic ministry in Colossians 1:28 and 'I decided to know nothing among you except Jesus Christ and him crucified' (1 Cor. 2:2) is his watchword. Moreover, we are all aware of the enormous ignorance of even the basic elements of the gospel in contemporary western culture and so the call to evangelism is vital and urgent. Surely then our preaching should reflect that, shouldn't it? Yes, but …! Not every passage of Scripture expounds the gospel, if by that we mean the substitutionary death of the Lord Jesus on the cross. Of course, the cross is the heart of God's grace in the gospel, but if my passage does not explicitly deal with that, the question for the preacher becomes, 'Am I going to impose this on to the text, or expound the content of this revelation as God has chosen to give it?' Exposition or imposition? That is the title of a blog posted by John Piper on the 'Desiring God' website, with the sub-title 'How gospel-centred preaching can go wrong'.[1]

In his article John Piper affirms that, in all his decades of preaching, his mind-set was never 'how can I preach the gospel from this text?' His concern was rather to discover the reality which the writer intended to communicate to his original readers and then to apply that reality to our own experience. Exposition, not imposition, honours the functional authority of Scripture, not just as a doctrinal position but in daily life and practice. Piper's advice is that instead of building the sermon <u>towards</u> the cross, build it <u>on</u> the cross. For example, when preaching an ethical passage from the epistles the writer's purpose is to produce godly behaviour in the believers, but the imperatives would be weakened by 'inserting the substitutionary atonement at critical moments when the emphasis should be falling on the urgency of obedience, because that's the urgency of the text'. The climax of the sermon should not be to pass over the imperatives, which we fail to fulfil, by going to the atoning death on the cross and ending by rejoicing that Jesus has carried our debt for us. That is gloriously true, but it is not the writer's purpose at this point. The authority of Scripture is in fact undermined if we leave the imperatives hanging, without reference to our obedience. The gospel is actually the starting point on which the applications are built, rather than an imposed climax which fails to expound the writer's intention.

---

1. Posted on 28 June 2020 on www.desiringgod.org

A second tool which is essential, but never exclusive, is that of rigorous exegesis. There can be no effective preaching without it, but if it becomes an end in itself the church will be in danger of becoming merely a lecture theatre. Hard work at the grammar, vocabulary, structure and context of the text to be preached is an essential foundation for everything else; but that is only the beginning. Good theological training will rightly establish accurate exegesis as indispensable, but preaching is not the same context as an academic seminar. Real preaching engages the heart as well as the mind, yet I have often spoken to Christians of considerable experience and maturity, who lament that the Biblical preaching they hear regularly may stimulate the intellect, but has nothing for the heart. 'Sola exegesis' was not one of the Reformation watchwords. Biblical exposition should communicate at every level of the personality – mind, heart and will. As one retired pastor put it to me, 'I would like to say to the younger preachers that you don't have to convince us that it's true; we already believe that. But we're having more than a bit of trouble living it out and that's where we need some help!'

Or, as another older Christian wrote anonymously, 'I have left church more times than I could count feeling empty at a spiritual level ... I have longed to <u>feel</u> something. To be moved to weep over my sin, marvel at God's greatness, leap for joy at His grace, to be led out in the sermon and taken to a place I did not know before, to grow. But instead it has all been so inoffensive and nice.' Before we are tempted to write that off as 'emotionalism', we should think again. No one is advocating the sort of manipulative controls that play upon the emotions in order to produce a reaction engendered by the preacher. We can all see through that sort of preaching and want no more of it. But emotion is different from emotionalism. God reveals Himself to us as an emotional being – He grieves, He is angry, He rejoices, He loves. His Word will inevitably reveal His many-faceted nature to us and we are made in His image, as emotional beings too. Many of us have been reared in a culture that dislikes 'wearing one's heart on one's sleeve' and perhaps over-values emotional reserve, but if exegesis is the only tool we use, our preaching is likely to become as one critic put it, 'icily regular, faultily faultless and splendidly dull.'

The third danger is an over-emphasis on systematic theology. Once again, this is an essential tool in the preacher's kit-bag, since in essence it is the outworking of the Biblical principle, rediscovered in the Reformation, that Scripture interprets Scripture. Systematics aims to bring varied Biblical references on a particular theme or issue together and by harmonising them, since they each have the one divine author, to come to a balanced overview of the whole Bible's perspective. This ensures that the preacher does not interpret one passage as *against* another, or exclusively emphasise the aspect of the issue covered in the passage he is expounding, as though there were no other Scriptural guides to its 'whole Bible' meaning. For the preacher, systematics is a valuable servant, but a dangerous master. The reason is that if it becomes the dominant tool we use, our sermons will tend to become thematic rather than expository, discursive rather than rooted in the text and therefore inclined towards the abstract and theoretical, rather than the concrete and practical. It will tend to greater interest in the problematic and controversial issues, often at the expense of practical down-to-earth godliness. The New Testament is not without its warnings about promoting 'speculations' and 'vain dissension' (1 Tim. 1:4-6), 'irreverent babble and contradictions of what is falsely called "knowledge"' (1 Tim. 6:20, 2 Tim. 2:16). By contrast, Paul reminds Timothy that, 'The aim of our charge is love that issues from a pure heart and a good conscience and a sincere faith' (1 Tim. 1:5).

Of course there is 'the pattern of sound words', the healthy apostolic teaching, 'the good deposit' (2 Tim. 1:13-14), 'the faith that was once for all delivered to the saints' (Jude v. 3), which the faithful pastor-teacher must always guard and propagate. Error is undermined by 'the open statement of the truth' (2 Cor. 4:2) and that is an essential requirement of the under-shepherd's teaching as he guards God's flock. But that is what the consistent, faithful, week-by-week exposition of the Biblical text achieves. God did not gift us an encyclopaedia of systematic theology, but the infinite variety of the Biblical genres, from the pens of widely differing individuals, across the centuries.

The function of systematic theology is extremely important, but the pulpit's teaching content is to be the exposition and application of the Bible text, rather than the theological text-book. Sermons based on systematics are also very difficult to do well. Because they are necessarily selective they tend to place the preacher, rather than the Bible, in the driving seat, since he will inevitably have to choose what to include or exclude; but on what grounds will he do that? The preacher's framework can easily take over at this point and he can become repetitive and predictable, especially as he becomes more set in his ways through age. There is also danger that the sermon will resemble a paper-chase through the Bible, which may be difficult for the hearers to engage with, so that sometimes it appears that the concordance rather than the Bible is shaping the preaching.

The final valuable tool which can unbalance the preacher is that of Biblical Theology. That title has been used in a number of different ways, but I am using it to cover the unveiling of the grand story-line, or metanarrative, of the whole Bible from Genesis to Revelation, moving from creation to the new creation. Again, this is a wonderful help to the expositor. It enables him to set his text in the context of the whole of Scripture. Where does this passage fit into the whole spectrum of God's self-revelation? It focuses on the pivotal hinge of history, with the coming of the Lord Jesus Christ into our world to accomplish God's great rescue mission. In the Old Testament it discovers the multitude of events and explanations which prepare the way for the coming of the Messiah, the Lord's anointed. So it directs us to Christ as the centre and fulfilment of God's redemptive and new creation purposes, as the Kingdom of God bursts into human history. Then it points us forward through His triumphant resurrection and ascension, to His return in power and glory to bring in the fulness of His eternal Kingdom in the new heavens and the new earth. For very many Christians the discovery of Biblical Theology, in recent years, has enabled them to see the Bible as a whole, in an entirely new perspective, has deepened their confidence in the veracity and integrity of Scripture and has provided the means of integrating the message of the two testaments. It is a hugely valuable tool, for which we should rightly be very thankful.

Where things go wrong is when it becomes the dominant principle in our sermons. Here the problem is where the intellectual fascination of tracking developments and discerning patterns takes over as the preacher's predominant concern. Many of the links depend upon typology, which is another wonderful Biblical tool, but the use of which can be notoriously subjective, unless it is validated by Scripture itself. Because both testaments are the revelation of the only true and living God operating throughout on the same principles, because of His unchanging nature, typology seeks to discover this continuity by identifying the parallels or correspondences between the old and the new. In his informative treatment of this theme John Goldingay writes that, 'Types are events, persons or institutions which are or become symbols of something brought about later which is analogous to, yet more glorious than, the original.'[2] He summarises that 'the heightening is a matter of the New Testament making clearer or more explicit what was allusive or implicit in the Old Testament.' The danger is that preachers, tempted to prove their intellectual athleticism or personal ingenuity, can become side tracked by the desire to discover (or create!) connections and links which no-one else has 'seen'. The effect can be dramatic, as the rabbit is pulled out of the hat, but the question is that once it is out what do you do with it? What is its take-away value?

---

2. John Goldingay 'Approaches to Old Testament Interpretation'; IVP Apollos, Leicester, 1990, see chapter 4; pp. 101-107.

The other problem is with what I call 'trampoline preaching'. Here the Old Testament text is bounced on in order to hasten the trajectory to the New Testament fulfilment. This means that the Old Testament is used merely as a means to an end and is rarely allowed to breathe its own air, to speak its own language, or to fulfil its own specific role as a unique part of the divine revelation. As one congregation member said to me about such preaching, 'We know it is going to get to the gospel. It's just a matter of whether it takes us five or twenty minutes to make it!' And that sort of predictability and sameness punctures any expectations of freshness which the hearers might have entertained. Perhaps the problem comes not only from the tool's over-use, but also from it not being applied in the most helpful way. The question that tends to be encouraged is, 'Where is Jesus in this text?' This can seem to be a valid application of the Biblical Theology tool, but I wonder whether it is the best question to ask, since it tends to put the emphasis on 'finding' a hidden Jesus, or, in desperation, smuggling Him in to a particular verse. We are then back to imposition, rather than exposition. For myself, I have found it more helpful to ask, 'What difference does it make to this text that Jesus has come?' This recognises the fulfilment motif, but it uses the later revelation as the interpretative key to the earlier, rather than trying to construct a connection from the earlier, which may owe more to the preacher's ingenuity than to the divine inspiration.

A skilled craftsman will always value his tools, keep them in tip-top condition and use them with wisdom and care. But they are only a means to an end-product which he is constructing. He may be delighted to own them and enjoy the fulfilment of using them, but it is what they enable him to produce that is the point of the whole exercise. So with the great tools we have been examining, the best way to ensure that they do not dominate or imbalance our preaching is to keep the ultimate purpose of their use clearly at the centre of the whole process. It has been well said that the Bible is God preaching God to us, because it is first and foremost His self-revelation, before its application to the multitude of our human issues and challenges, to which it provides the answer. We are prone in our preaching to put the cart before the horse. We tend to assume that we can take the doctrine of God as 'read', knowledge which almost everyone has in place. But wherever we meet Christians who say, 'I like to think that God ...' or 'I'm sure that God would never ...' who are clearly operating in the context of their own desires or preferences, rather than the teaching of Scripture, we are made to realise how uninstructed, or unresponsive, we can be. Simply demonstrating our expertise in using the tools does not in itself guarantee the accomplishment of our goals.

The Bible itself teaches us the importance of having the foundation truths revisited and refreshed as the heart of a teaching ministry. The vocabulary of 'remembering' is very strongly emphasised in the New Testament writings. Peter surely represents this common apostolic concern, when he tells his readers that he intends always to remind them of these foundational truths and consequent character qualities, 'though you know them and are established in the truth that you have.' As long as he is able, he will seek 'to stir you up by way of reminder' (2 Pet. 1:12-13). This is not to be misunderstood as a call to the endless rehearsal of the most basic information, in a repetitive and formulaic way. The letter to the Hebrews is quite clear that there is a time to be leaving 'the elementary doctrine of Christ and go on to maturity' (Heb. 6:1). The author's rebuke is that his readers need someone to teach them again 'the basic principles of the oracles of God. You need milk, not solid food' (Heb. 5:12). The principle here is that there can be no progress to maturity if the basics are not in place and sometimes they do have to be refreshed and renewed. This is because we become 'dull of hearing' and our spiritual memories are so short. However, Biblical remembering is not just the recall of information, but a call to consistent living on the basis of the truth already received.

A key verse in understanding this principle is 2 Timothy 2:8, where Paul exhorts the pastor-teacher Timothy, 'Remember Jesus Christ, risen from the dead, the offspring of David, as preached in my gospel'. Timothy did not need to be reminded about who Jesus was, His genealogy, His resurrection or the contents of the apostolic gospel. He had not forgotten these foundation facts. But he did need to meet the challenges of the preceding verses (to be a good soldier, a diligent athlete and a hard working farmer) by acting on the truth that he already knew (2 Tim. 2:3-7). As he kept these great gospel realities in mind, he would recall the demonstration of God's power in keeping His Word, raising His Son and being the dependable provider of all that Timothy would need to fulfil his ministry, in the challenging context of Ephesus. When Jesus instituted the Lord's supper and taught us,

'Do this in remembrance of me' (Luke 22:19), it was not in case the cross might somehow be forgotten, but so that His people would constantly be recalled to live in the light of His sacrificial, atoning death, lives of gratitude and holiness, 'feeding on him in our hearts by faith'.

As we go on in ministry we all develop favourite Biblical 'watering holes' to which we often return when we need the refreshment of being reminded of the unchanging realities at the heart of our lives and ministries. With regard to teaching the doctrine of God, one of my favourite passages is Isaiah 51:12-16. Set at the start of a new section of the book which will take us to the final servant song in the magisterial 53rd chapter, these words are God's response to Isaiah's prayer in 51:9, 'Awake, awake put on strength, O arm of the Lord; awake as in days of old.' His plea expresses a longing for deliverance from the exile which Isaiah has been prophesying, but its urgent summons, 'Wake up, Lord', reveals something about His servant's forgetfulness of the true nature of the God whom he is addressing. The paragraph begins, therefore, with God speaking, 'I, I am he who comforts you; who are you that you are afraid of man who dies, of the son of man who is made like grass, and have forgotten the LORD, your Maker?' There, in one sentence, is the key to the fears and frustrations of Isaiah and the people he serves. They have forgotten who their God really is and that is why the fear of men has filled their minds and paralysed their actions. He is still the LORD (Yahweh – the covenant God who never changes) and His covenant is still in place, however much the present circumstances seem to question, or even deny it.

The pastoral and transformational intention of the passage is already becoming clear, and as such it provides a model for any Bible teacher dealing with a similar situation. Israel's thinking and actions are to be changed, not by exhortation to pull themselves together and trust, but by being fed with the glorious aspects of the character of God (the object of their trust) which he expounds in the rest of the paragraph. Teaching must always come before exhortation. And what great teaching is here! In verse 12, God declares Himself to be the source of their 'comfort' in terms of His loving, personal relationship with them which brings strength, new life and energy to His despairing people, as He promised back in 40:1. In verse 13, He is 'Yahweh, your Maker' and in verse 16, Yahweh, your God'. In the first case the pronoun 'your' is plural, referring to the whole people of God (Zion) and in the second, singular, which implies that it is referring to Isaiah himself or to the suffering servant. The reference in verse 13 to 'your Maker' is therefore best understood not as simply indicating the creation of the human race, but with reference to the covenant people, whom God brought into existence through the deliverance from Egypt in the Passover and constituted as His 'holy nation' at Mount Sinai. They have forgotten that He is the creator of the entire cosmos (heavens and earth, v. 13) and therefore is the sovereign Lord over all the mortal human beings of which they are currently in fear, 'continually all the day' (v. 13). Their enemies are merely men who die, who are made like grass (v. 12). From a human perspective 'the wrath of the oppressor' is a terrifying reality which threatens destruction of the people of God (v. 13b), but that is the perspective which forgets who the LORD really is. Verse 14 teaches us that He releases His captive people, that He preserves their life, sustaining and nourishing them. So, we learn that we fear men when we forget God, when we fail to reckon on His 'otherness', His supreme power and authority, coupled to His faithful, covenant promises.

In verse 15, He declares, 'I am the Lord, your God, who stirs up the sea so that its waves roar – the LORD of hosts is his name'. This is a far greater assurance than the single thought that however much the sea may roar the Lord is able to control it (true though that is – see Mark 4:35-41). Here we are told that it is Yahweh who wills the storm and produces the raging seas. He is 'the LORD of hosts', often translated as 'the LORD Almighty'. Commenting on this frequently used title in Isaiah, Alec Motyer writes that it 'represents two nouns in apposition, (lit.) 'The LORD [who is] hosts'. In other words, to think of the Lord is to think of power and resource unbounded ('hosts' being a 'plural of diversity' and indicating 'every sort of').[3] This is exactly the perspective we need to keep reaffirming to our congregations, as we teach the much needed doctrine of God. And where better to teach it from than a series in Isaiah 40-55?

Finally, in verse 16, the concept of divine sovereignty over the heavens and the earth (repeated almost exactly from verse 13) is revisited, but this time with special reference to the assurance and security this truth gives to the one who ministers God's words, 'covered in the shadow of my hand'. The final clause overflows this covenant protection, from the servant to the whole community of

3. 'The Prophecy of Isaiah,' by J. A. Motyer; IVP Leicester, 1993; p. 44.

God's covenant people (Zion) in the reaffirmed promise
from the lips of their covenant Lord in person, 'You are
my people'. With these certainties recalled and believed,
what room can there be for the fear of men, however
intimidating they may currently seem to be? No wonder
the next verse turns the plea to God to awaken (v. 9) back
on to the people, as God responds, on the basis of what He
has just revealed to them, 'Wake yourself, wake yourself,
stand up, O Jerusalem' (v. 17). Biblical remembering is
always with a view to positive action in the light of revealed
truth. As one of the old hymns puts it, 'Tell me the story
often, for I forget so soon'.

Here, then, is an emphasis which can never lead to any
imbalance, because it is not merely a tool in the preacher's
hand, but the dominating content of the whole Biblical
revelation, which must become the supreme concern of all
his preaching. Quoting Cotton Mather (1663–1728), the
New England puritan pastor, who wrote over 400 books,
John Piper recalls that Mather wrote, 'The great design and
intention of the office of a Christian preacher [is] to restore
the throne and dominion of God in the souls of men'. This
powerful sentence comes from Mather's exposition of
Romans 10:14-15, in which the content of the good news
to be heralded is established, by Paul's quotation from the
very next chapter of Isaiah, 'How beautiful are the feet of
those who preach the good news' (Isa. 52:7). That verse
describes the gospel as 'peace, good news of happiness,
salvation', but concludes with a summary of its contents
in three words, 'Your God reigns'. It is the exploration and
exposition of this greatest theme in all the Scriptures which
ensures the preaching of the good news in some aspect of

its multi-faceted glory in every sermon or talk. Relating Mather's observation to our contemporary context, John Piper comments that this phrase conveys God's 'absolute creator rights over this world and everyone in it'. That will demand both the proclamation of His wrath against all rebellion and also the declaration of a 'full and free amnesty ... signed by the blood of his Son', for all who will turn and call on Him for mercy. He concludes, 'The implication for preaching is plain: When God sent his emissaries to declare, 'Your God reigns!' his aim is not to constrain men's submission by an act of raw authority, his aim is to ravish our affections with irresistible displays of glory.'[4]

Is that not something to work and pray for? Not simply to be competent practitioners with the tools God has given us, though we must never underestimate their importance; but to be those who seek to be the channels by which God, the Holy Spirit, calls our hearers to glad submission as the expression of our love, in response to His 'irresistible displays' of His glory and grace.

---

4. 'The Supremacy of God in Preaching,' by John Piper; Baker Books, Grand Rapids, Michigan, U.S.A., 1990; pp. 22-25.

10.

Preaching law and liberty rightly

Why do we Christians seem so easily to lose our appetite to grow in godliness of life and character? We start off with enthusiasm and zeal, but we all know how quickly this can degenerate into a humdrum, almost mechanistic, experience of Christian living. We still believe the same things and even continue our practices of Bible-reading and prayer, but there seems to be no great desire for growth, or indeed for God. Many Christians seem to think of their daily life after conversion in terms of seeking to imitate Christ, but often without much enthusiasm or effectiveness. In terms of Romans 8:30, what should life look like between being justified and being glorified? We all know how easy it is to settle down to a level of outwardly apparently godly behaviour, which satisfies the standards and norms of the sub-cultural peer group to which we belong, but which actually lacks any dynamic for real progress and development.

Sometimes our preaching can contribute to this state of affairs by setting the bar too high. Of course we want to motivate ourselves and our hearers to be the best that we can be for Christ and the Kingdom, but if our illustrations of that are always of exceptional examples, what we might call 'super saints', who seem to have reached a superior level to the 'normal', one of two responses may occur. On the one hand for many, the target may seem so unattainable that they decide not to enter the competition. They don't have the time or the energy. 'It's great that there are "super saints", but I'm not in their league.' On the other, it may precipitate a restless quest to find the silver bullet or the magic key to resolve all the difficulties. And whatever they decide it to be, this then tends to produce a new elitism, which becomes fashionable for a while, until the crash-landing that must happen because the superior level cannot be sustained.

In both cases the fundamental mistake seems to be in thinking that the righteousness, or godly maturity, for which in our best moments all believers long, has to be found in us – our commitment, our efforts, our consistency. We have lost sight of Christ and the fact that the only maturity or godliness that we have is in Christ alone, since it is only through our faith union with Him that we become 'partakers of the divine nature' (2 Pet. 1:4) and that all the riches of His perfect righteousness can become ours. The true motivation to holy living then is to become what we already are; to work out in practice what God has already worked in us. However, it is not unusual for the challenge to grow in godliness to produce or resort to a religion of moralism or legalism, by which we are tempted to try to justify ourselves before God. And it is at this point that the wise pastor-teacher is especially aware of a mechanism which we might call 'pendulum-swing'. In any congregation reactions can develop unhealthily against emphases which are in themselves off centre. The temptation is to try to correct an unhealthy imbalance of the pendulum by pushing it in the opposite direction. This produces a stronger push-back and as the pendulum swings backwards and forwards, what gets lost is the Biblical standard. The way to correct the extremes is to recall everyone to the Biblical perpendicular, which requires patient teaching and careful instruction.

One of the areas which requires most careful handling is the question of the place of the law in the life of the believer. As we rightly elevate the person and work of Christ and our total dependence on grace, we need to take care that this does not tip over into a rejection of the law. Otherwise, it becomes easy to say that the Old Testament was about law, but the New is about grace and to oppose them to each other. For example, when we read the demands of the Old Testament moral law, which of course reflect God's unchanging character, we should not slip into the view that because Jesus has perfectly fulfilled all this for us, in our place, we no longer need to consider its instruction to be relevant. This would be to render large swathes of Old Testament revelation as redundant.

Certainly, the issue of the right place of the Torah (instruction) in the life of the Christian has been a matter of considerable contention since the time of the Reformation, because the law clearly could not deliver from the guilt or power of sin. However, over the centuries a broad consensus has developed among Biblical Christians that while, unlike Israel, we do not live in a theocracy, the law still serves as a template for human society in terms of behavioural ideals built on the character of God, the creator. This role is sometimes referred to as the Maker's instructions, as for example in the Ten Commandments. From this stems the second purpose of the law, which is to delineate the failure of every human being to keep God's commands and so to drive us to Christ for His forgiveness, through the cross. Thirdly, for those thus rescued, through faith in Christ, the law describes and directs the path of holy living or godliness. There is a real and present danger that we lose these positive and essential benefits of the law in contemporary evangelical preaching under the false supposition that what I have just described is 'legalism'.

Nothing could be further from the reality. The essence of legalism is to stress that obedience to the law becomes more than the evidence of the reality of faith, in the fruit of a godly life. 'If you love me,' Jesus said, 'you will keep my commandments' (John 14:15). As the apostle John teaches us, 'For this is the love of God that we keep his commandments. And his commandments are not burdensome' (1 John 5:3). What legalism does is to elevate this obedience to become a necessary constituent element of justifying faith. We are not then saved by grace alone through faith alone, but by faith and our own obedience. The obedience which is the evidence of faith (James 2:20-26) then in practice becomes salvific so that I am saved by Jesus plus my keeping of the law. And, as always, this 'Jesus plus' theology is actually a 'Jesus minus' theology, because faith in the completed work of Christ is effectively regarded as insufficient. This mistake was the essence of Pharisaism. Among Christians it creates inward-looking, morbid introspection, leading to deprivation of assurance and joy, and if unchecked it has the power to divide and ultimately destroy whole Christian communities. So, it is very important for a teacher to be clear about one's understanding of the place of the law in the life of Christian liberty, if we are seeking to promote Biblical maturity. If the way in to the Christian life is the restoration of the relationship of the believer with God, on the sole grounds of Christ's death and resurrection, then the way on, as the image of God is being restored in the believer, cannot be on any other basis.

The cause of many of these difficulties is the failure to put the law into its whole Bible perspective and so to misunderstand its original nature and purpose. The key passage to understand here is the narrative in Exodus 19 concerning the giving of the law at Sinai. Three months out of Egypt, God leads His redeemed people to meet Him at the mountain, where He had first met with Moses (Exod. 3:1, 12) and commissioned him for the exodus. Here God will give His people the law, the tabernacle and the sacrificial system, for their journey to Canaan and conquest of the land. But first God reminds them of what He has already done for them. 'You yourselves have seen what I did to the Egyptians, and how I bore you on eagles' wings and brought you to myself' (Exod. 19:4). They have experienced His victory over the Egyptians in the Passover deliverance and at the Red Sea. He has lifted them out of their slavery and brought them, not just to Sinai, but 'to myself'. They are already in relationship with Him, already restored to a reconciled God, since the blood of the Passover lambs has turned away His wrath. What He then requires of Israel is for them to live in the light of this already established reality. 'Now therefore, if you will indeed obey my voice and keep my covenant, you shall be my treasured possession among all peoples, for all the earth is mine' (v. 5).

This is not God striking a bargain with Israel. The promise of verse 5 is already stated as an accomplished fact in verse 4. That is why when the Ten Commandments are given in the next chapter they are preceded by the same statement of the already existing relationship. 'I am the LORD your God, who brought you out of the land of Egypt, out of the house of slavery' (Exod. 20:2). What the law provides is the detailed instruction as to how they can possess what God is providing. It is by hearing God's words ('my voice') and responding in covenant obedience. This covenant relationship is the provision of God's grace to enable them not only to know what to do but to be able to appropriate the means, through the sacrificial provision He makes for their failures. The blessing that will follow concerns their unique identity as 'a kingdom of priests and a holy (set apart) nation' (v. 6).

The law of God comes from God Himself, expressing His character and as the channel of His grace, by which the covenant relationship between God and Israel is sealed. Some commentators have suggested that much of the law is expressed in a negative form ('You shall not …') because its focus is on what would destroy the relationship created by grace, so that is what is prohibited. The law is to be seen as the divinely-given pattern of life provided for those who have been redeemed by the blood of the Passover lamb. God brings Israel to Sinai, to reveal Himself more fully to them in the law. He will instruct them how to live within covenant grace, so as to enjoy the promised covenant blessings and that pattern is not different in the new covenant. It is hugely important that we recognise and teach that the law was never intended to be a ladder to climb, by which human beings might vainly attempt to reach God. It is not God putting into Israel's hands the responsibility for reversing the effects of the fall, only to show them that they cannot do it, so that they are prepared for a deliverer. He does not play games like that with His covenant people. All through the Old Testament it is the combination of God's Word in the Scriptures (and especially through the prophets), and God's provision in the sacrifices which enable faithful believers to enjoy a real living relationship with their holy God. 'Blessed is the one whose transgression is forgiven, whose sin is covered. Blessed is the man against whom the LORD counts no iniquity, and in whose spirit there is no deceit' (Ps. 32:1-2).

Once we begin to see how the law functions within the perspective of the whole Old Testament, we are in a much better position to explore the key question, 'But what difference does it make that Jesus has come?' Not surprisingly it is in Matthew's gospel, arguably the most Jewish of the four, that we find the answer spelt out most fully. The first of the five major blocks of teaching in Matthew, which we call the Sermon on the Mount, occupies chapters 5-7 and is often described as the manifesto of God's kingdom. But it is the first four chapters which provide us with the context in which we must interpret its application. Clearly, Matthew sees the teaching and its context as the fulfilment of the promise of Isaiah 2:2-3. 'It shall come to pass in the latter days that the mountain of the house of the LORD shall be established as the highest of the mountains and shall be lifted up above the hills; and all nations shall flow to it and many peoples shall come, and say: "Come let us go up to the mountain of the LORD, to the house of the God of Jacob, that he may teach us his ways and that we may walk in his paths".' However, Matthew has already alerted us to the fact that this is not merely a replay of Sinai. Immediately before the sermon, the unit 4:12-16 indicates that Jesus' ministry, just beginning, is the fulfilment of another great Isaianic prophecy that will impact 'Galilee of the Gentiles' with the 'great light' of the one who will inhabit David's throne 'to establish it and to uphold it with justice and with righteousness from this time forth and forevermore' (Isa. 9:6-7).

Then by way of introduction to the sermon itself, Jesus is presented in 4:17 as preaching the good news of the Kingdom, a phrase repeated in 4:23 describing the heart of His Galilean ministry. But in between (4:18-22) Jesus calls the Galilean fishermen, as His first disciples, to a radical change of life-style, leaving all to follow Him. His first kingdom action (4:19) is therefore a blend of summons or command ('Follow me'), immediately accompanied by a word of promise or grace ('and I will make you fishers of men'). That was the structure of the first giving of the law at Sinai, as indeed it was in the call of Abram, right at the beginning of God's salvation plan. The word of command, 'Go from your country to the land that I will show you' already has within it the promise, which is then expanded in the covenantal blessing, 'And I will make of you a great nation, and I will bless you and make your name great, so that you will be a blessing' (Gen. 12:1-2). That is always the pattern within the covenant – believe the promises and obey the commands. That is the way to blessing and that is to be the pattern within the new covenant community which Jesus has come to create. The revolutionary teaching of the sermon will be central, but is to be understood in the context of promise, as in the Beatitudes (Matt. 5:2-12).

The opening chapters of Matthew's gospel continually stress the fulfilment motif as the person of Jesus is introduced. He is the son of David, the son of Abraham (1:1-17), the fulfilment of the Isaiah 7:14 promise in His virgin birth, Jesus the Saviour, Immanuel, God with us (1:21-23) and like Joseph (Gen. 50:20) taken to Egypt for His preservation and the salvation of many (2:13-15). Called out of Egypt as God's Son, He fulfils Hosea 11:1 (2:15) and as He is about to begin His ministry, John the Baptist proclaims the true end of the exile (3:1-3), as prophesied in Isaiah 40:3, which culminates in the voice from heaven declaring at the baptism, 'This is my beloved Son, with whom I am well pleased' (3:17). Challenged and tested by the devil in the wilderness (4:1-11), He emerges as the proven son, perfect in obedience, where Israel so repeatedly failed. So it is against this profoundly significant fulfilment background that we hear Him declare to His disciples, 'Do not think that I have come to abolish the Law or the Prophets; I have not come to abolish them but to fulfil them' (5:17).

The Beatitudes come first because they indicate His fulfilment of the great prophecy of Isaiah 61:1-2, which, in Luke's account of the early ministry (Luke 4:16-21), Jesus attributes to Himself as He begins His public ministry in the synagogue at Nazareth. He is the anointed servant of God appointed to bring the good news of the Lord's favour (grace) to the needy. The blessings of the heavenly kingdom are already breaking in, but they are for those who know they are spiritual bankrupts, yet who 'hunger and thirst for righteousness' (5:6). Always beyond the reach of even the most devout, this righteousness is now proclaimed as God's gracious gift, in fulfilment of Isaiah's prophetic rejoicing in God, 'for he has clothed me with the garments of salvation; he has covered me with the robe of righteousness' (Isa. 61:10). The demand for righteousness is not abolished, but it comes now as the gift of God's grace to all who submit to God's king, the fulfilment of all the prophetic promises. A new era is dawning for the whole human race, as the citizens of the eternal kingdom become 'the salt of the earth, the light of the world, a city set on a hill that cannot be hidden' (5:13-14).

So what does all this essential foundation work mean for our understanding of Jesus' declaration about the law? He has come to fulfil all the Old Testament prophecies of the Messianic deliverer, but also to be the perfect and unflawed demonstration of a human life lived in perfect obedience to the Father, which is the fulfilment of the law. However, this fulfilment does not contradict the continuing validity of the law, until the final coming of the eternal Kingdom ('until all is accomplished' 5:18). Nevertheless, the revolutionary difference is that the law is now to be interpreted and applied by Jesus Himself as the law giver. So in the examples which follow (5:21-48) the same formula is applied time after time. 'You have heard that it was said … but I say to you.' That is never a negation of the law and its demand, but a re-interpretation in the light of the incoming kingdom of heaven, which intensifies and internalises the original purpose of the commandments. In David E. Holwerda's insightful analysis, he affirms, 'This greater righteousness requires conformity to the entire will of God, rather than the observance of minimal standards derived from the letter of the commandments treated in isolation.' He goes on to explain that the hermeneutic Jesus uses to expound the commandments is the law of love – for God and for neighbour.[1] This is what Jesus means about righteousness that exceeds that of the scribes and Pharisees (5:20). His penetrating critique of their distorted legalism focuses on their addition of so many minutiae that the central concept of God's grace in the giving of the law is entirely removed.

There is one further major area of study to which we must turn if we are rightly to handle God's Word of truth in the application of the law to the Christian life. That is to ask how the apostles and the early church saw the issue and what their practice became. Here the classic text is Paul's letter to the Galatians, probably his earliest extant epistle, in which we soon realise what a crucial and explosive issue the relationship between the law and the gospel was from the very beginning. The opening of the letter immediately expresses how scandalised Paul is by those who have come into the Galatian churches peddling 'a different gospel', which is no gospel at all (Gal. 1:6-7). They are to be 'accursed', because there is and can only ever be one gospel, which, as Paul affirms, he received

---

1. 'Jesus and Israel,' David E. Holwerda; Eerdmans, Grand Rapids, 1995; p. 133 et al.

through a direct revelation of Jesus Christ (1:12). He had never been dependent on the Jerusalem church, either for his message or their approval. So, when he was led by revelation to visit Jerusalem and met with the church's leaders, James and Peter and John, they added nothing to Paul's understanding. Rather, they recognised that he had been entrusted with the same one gospel, to preach to the Gentiles, as they had to the Jews (2:1-10). However, right from the beginning of the letter Paul identifies the conflict in terms of law versus liberty. He describes the motivation of the law party, which he encountered in Jerusalem, as 'false brothers ... who slipped in to spy out our freedom that we have in Christ Jesus, so that they might bring us into slavery' (2:4). Paul's shorthand description of them is 'the circumcision party' (2:12), since they were seeking to impose the requirements of the old covenant upon the Gentile members of the new, through food laws and other observances, right up to circumcision. As 6:12 makes plain, 'they would force you to be circumcised'.

For Paul, this is a fundamental distortion of the gospel, which will ultimately destroy it, because it adds law-keeping as a necessary requirement for salvation. Such teaching effectively diminishes Christ's work and demeans His person, because it implies that He is insufficient as the saviour of all who come to Him through faith alone, by grace alone. However, it is significant that in the letter Paul presents the issue as a conflict, not just between law and gospel, but between slavery and freedom and, later, between the flesh and the Spirit. When, at Antioch, Peter separated himself from eating with Gentiles 'fearing the circumcision party', who must have been strong and very influential in Jerusalem and so leading all the other Jews, including Barnabas, to follow him. Paul's opposition to him was based on the fact that 'their conduct was not in step with the truth of the gospel' (2:14). Three times in 2:15-16, Paul reaffirms that 'a person (whether Jew or Gentile) is not justified by works of the law, but through faith in Jesus Christ'. For Paul this is not just a doctrine to be believed and proclaimed, but a freedom to be experienced and at all costs defended.

It is vital that these realities are built into the lives of those whom we seek to teach, so that they (and we) are never tempted to look anywhere else, least of all to any outward conformity to the law, for our justification, 'because by works of the law no one will be justified' (2:16), or ever could be. Galatians is a great text from which to teach these realities and although this is not the place for a detailed exposition of the book, it is certainly to be commended as one essential part of a balanced Biblical teaching programme. The attraction, then and now, of going back to the slavery of works religion, seems to be that it enables us to walk by sight and not by faith. We set up external standards, which we can (mostly) keep and then we have a discernible 'righteousness', which can be observed and which removes the gospel requirement that we walk by faith in the promises of God. This generates pride in the legalist that he has attained the standard, coupled with disdain for those who have not. The argument of the circumcision party seems to have been that justification by faith alone removes the visible distinction between the righteous and the unrighteous and with it the motivation to godliness. Christ then becomes 'a servant of sin', but

Paul's vigorous riposte is that the sin is in fact to rebuild what the gospel has shown to be ineffective and redundant and what was torn down through the cross, which is the attempt to be justified by works of the law.

There follows a key principle in understanding, living and teaching the Christian life, succinctly expressed by Paul. 'For through the law I died to the law, so that I might live to God' (2:19). Living to God had always been Paul's goal before his conversion, which he had tried to accomplish by his extreme zeal (1:14) including his persecution of the infant church. But when he was confronted by the risen Christ, on the road to Damascus, he came to realise that the law could never deal with his transgressions; indeed, as a way to life it was a dead-end. So Paul died to the law as a way to life, which he then explains more fully in one of the most famous verses in all of his writings. 'I have been crucified with Christ. It is no longer I who live, but Christ who lives in me. And the life I now live in the flesh I live by faith in the Son of God, who loved me and gave himself for me' (2:20). The death of Christ and the risen life of Christ are both integral to the apostle's experience. At the cross the old life of works-righteousness and its constant failure was dealt with once for all, as its penalty was met and its power broken by Christ's atoning sacrifice. As Paul puts it, the Son of God 'loved me and gave himself for me'. But the Christ who gave Himself for me at Calvary is the Christ who 'lives in me' now, so that this new life of gospel freedom, 'I live by faith in the Son of God'. It is faith, not works, that justifies and the way in to the Christian life is the way on as well. To think that one could live as a Christian any other way would be to nullify God's grace, 'for if justification were through the law, then Christ died for no purpose' (2:21). That is a devastating indictment of the law party. It should spell the end of all our petty legalistic additions to the gospel.

Chapters 3 and 4 contain the main argument of the letter, which we can only briefly sketch in here, but the great development of the basic thesis is to demonstrate that the new life of gospel liberty is made possible through the work of the Holy Spirit. Here for the Bible teacher is the foundational principle that progress in godliness is the fruit of the Spirit's work within, changing the believer from the inside out. The first outcome of the preaching of Christ crucified for the Galatians, as they heard the good news and responded by faith, was that they received the gift of the Holy Spirit (3:1-2). Neither the blessings of Calvary or Pentecost came through the law, which Paul now categorises, in contra-distinction to the Spirit, as 'the flesh' (3:3). Twice he reminds his readers that their spiritual existence depends on 'hearing with faith' (vv. 2 and 5), not works of the law, and by that they are proving themselves to be the true offspring of Abraham, 'the man of faith', and the fulfilment of the Genesis 12 promise (3:6-9). In the immediate context of the issues in Galatia, this introduction of Abraham is a master-stroke, as Paul moves on to his opponents' ground, the Old Testament, which he then proceeds to use to demolish their case on their own premises. There are four quotations from the Old Testament in 3:10-13, each of which undermines the idea that the law could ever justify and which culminate in the summary statement that 'in Christ Jesus the blessing of Abraham might come to the Gentiles, so that we might receive the promised Spirit through faith' (3:14). It is all there in that verse. The free grace of God blessing the Gentiles, not them assuming the burden of the law, meant that the gift of the Spirit is God's provision to overcome the flesh (5:16), not by the law, and this is received by faith and not produced by works.

From this point on in Galatians the gift and ministry of the Holy Spirit in the believer assumes centre-stage, as it must always do in our teaching of the Christian life. Sadly, it is an area in which 'charismatic' and 'non-charismatic' Christians have reacted against one another, by pushing the pendulum to extremes in their defence of their 'position', but in doing so have all too often ignored the Biblical perpendicular. For Paul, the gospel of grace is all about God's initiative in sending the remedy for human slavery to sin and the inability of the law to do anything other than condemn, which he expresses in two memorable, foundational statements. Firstly, 'God sent forth his Son, born of woman, born under the law, to redeem those who were under the law, so that we might receive adoption as sons' (4:4-5). Then, consequently, 'God has sent the Spirit of his Son into our hearts, crying "Abba! Father!"' (4:6). The gift of God's Son <u>for</u> us on the cross and the gift of God's Spirit <u>within</u> us to transform us from the inside out are the heart of the good news and the escape route from slavery to the law and the tyranny of the flesh.

For the last part of the letter the theme of freedom in the Spirit dominates, expounding the clarion call of 5:1. 'For freedom Christ has set us free; stand firm therefore, and do not submit again to a yoke of slavery.' It is the Spirit who makes us children of the promise, through the new birth of which He is the agent (4:28-29). It is the Spirit who stimulates our appetite and eager expectation of righteousness, by faith working through love (5:5-6). Walking by the Spirit, in His energy and power, is the only way to nullify the desires of the flesh (5:16), against which both the law and our own unaided efforts will always be in vain. It is the Spirit who empowers believers to do battle with the flesh and who leads us into the domain of freedom, not back under the inability of the law (5:17-18). It is the Spirit who produces His fruit in that mature Christian adulthood which is a portrait of Christ (5:22-23). So the Christian's calling is to 'walk by the Spirit', to keep in step with his desires and priorities, to bring our lives into conformity with God's will through our dependence on the Spirit's enabling strength and grace. And this matters supremely because 'the one who sows to the Spirit will from the Spirit reap eternal life' (6:8).

These are the truths which we need constantly to assimilate ourselves, to live by each day, and to make sure that we are teaching consistently to our hearers, so that these Biblical essentials become the foundations of our Christian experience. Because the law given at Sinai embodies the character of the God who gave it, which is unchanging, it will always provide us with the principles and examples of a life that is pleasing to God. But with the coming of the Lord Jesus the dynamic has changed. His fulfilment of the law and one offering of Himself, once for all, as the atoning sacrifice for sin, means that through faith in Him, like Paul, we have died to the law. Our hymn books are full of rejoicing in this reality but our heads need to be full of understanding and our hearts full of assurance and confidence, as we recognise the liberty into which God's grace has brought us. Keep reminding yourself and your hearers about it! Catherine Pennefather puts it with such simple but profound significance.

> *Thou hast fulfilled the law,*
> *And we are justified:*
> *Ours is the blessing, Thine the curse;*
> *We live, for Thou hast died.*[2]

When we are united to Christ, by faith in His person as the Son of God and in His work as our saviour, the Spirit of Christ enters the believer to occupy the whole of life and to begin His great, transforming work of forming Christ in us (Gal. 4:19). The Holy Spirit is the energising link between the Christ who is enthroned in the heavenlies and yet who dwells in our hearts by faith. He is the other 'helper', advocate, or comforter in the sense of strengthener (the Paraclete) whom Jesus promised (John 14:16) who represents Jesus wholly and completely, so that in fact Paul often uses the phrase 'in the Spirit' interchangeably with the phrase 'in Christ'. This is how our liberty is to be experienced and enjoyed. This is how the Jeremiah promise from God, to put His law within His people and write it on their hearts (Jer. 31:33) and the Ezekiel promise from God, to put His spirit within His people and cause them to walk in His statutes (Ezek. 36:27) are both fulfilled. For the Holy Spirit is God's gift to every Christian (Rom. 8:9), through whose ministry our union with Christ is understood and applied. We live in Christ,

---

2. The hymn 'Jesus, the sinner's Friend,' by Mrs Catherine Pennefather (1818–1893).

draw all our enabling from Christ and so, by His grace, our lives are dedicated to serving Him and responding in obedience to His kingly rule. The law can achieve none of these things; but it does reveal the character of the God who gave it and it does unfold the divinely given pattern of life for those who have been redeemed by the blood of the lamb. Far from being the enemy of the gospel, when it is rightly understood and used, it leads us to Christ, who Himself says to His followers, 'If you love me, you will keep my commandments' (John 14:15).

II.

Preaching that recognises God's work and ours

At the heart of all true Christian experience and conditioning all our considerations of pastoral theology lies the Biblical paradox of the divine and the human working together. It is there in our doctrine of Scripture as the breathed-out word of God, eternal and unchanging, but expressed through the lips and pens of human agents, each with their own stylistic characteristics. It is there supremely in the incarnation of our Lord Jesus Christ, 'begotten of his Father before all worlds, God of God, Light of Light ... being of one substance with the Father' and yet 'the Word became flesh and dwelt among us' (John 1:14). 'He was made man and was crucified for us. He suffered and was buried and the third day he rose again.'[1] Being both fully divine and fully human, He took upon Himself our human nature, emptying Himself of His dignity, but not of His deity. But who can separate the two?

Perhaps it is not surprising that many of the challenges and problems associated with teaching and living the

---

1. Quoted from the Nicene Creed.

Christian life centre around this foundational paradox. In salvation and in sanctification what is God's part and what is ours? How do the two agencies blend together in the practicalities of life? It is only too easy to fall off the tight-rope of the Biblical balance, by over-emphasising one aspect at the expense of the other. Many were taught in the past that the motto for Christian growth and fruitfulness was 'Let go and let God'. The positive aspect of this strap-line is that it recognises that only the power of God within the Christian can actually transform us progressively to become like Christ. But if human responsibility is excluded from the reckoning, we end up with what Jim Packer used to call 'hot tub religion' and others have labelled 'jacuzzi Christianity', where the responsibility to mortify the flesh is replaced by relaxing into the warm bubbles, thinking that God will do it all. I remember as a student being given a fluorescent card by some of my pietistic fellow students, which was to be kept on my desk and which read, 'Don't wrestle; just nestle'! On the other hand, others of us have been taught that the Christian life is an unremitting struggle in which our sinful nature guarantees our repeated failure and so our experience degenerates into a heavy burden of what actually begins to look like works religion, as if there were no transformative divine power to call upon.

But the genius of the New Testament is that it rejects the 'either/or' perspective and rejoices instead in the 'both/and'. So the apostle Paul exhorts the Philippians, 'Work out your own salvation with fear and trembling, for it is God who works in you, both to will and to work for his good pleasure' (Phil. 2:12-13). What God works in us, we are responsible to be working out in our lives. Peter makes the same point, with the same emphasis, in the major passage at the start of his second letter, 2 Peter 1:3-8. 'God's divine power has granted us everything we need for life and godliness ... For this very reason make every effort to add to your faith ... (This) will keep you from being ineffective or unfruitful in the knowledge of our Lord Jesus Christ.' The divine power combined with 'his precious and very great promises' (v. 4) are the means by which our responsibility to supplement our faith with all the qualities of Christ-likeness, which verses 5-7 expound, becomes possible. Both of these ingredients need to be held together, in balance, if we are to be truly Biblical in our teaching of the Christian life. So, let us explore in some key New Testament passages how the inspired apostolic authors teach both divine power and human responsibility.

The key concept is most often expressed in terms of our 'union with Christ' and since this is so clearly the central reality of true Christian experience it is logical that both the doctrinal foundation and the practical outworking should be given a great deal of coverage in the apostolic texts. There is a variety of prepositions used; 'in' Christ, 'unto', 'with', 'through', 'by', but always the foundational link is between the person and work of Christ and the experience of this in the life of the believer, from new birth to glorification. I have found great help in Constantine Campbell's excellent exegetical and theological study of the whole theme.[2] In seeking to define the nature of this union, he identifies four significant aspects. The first and major ingredient is the concept of the union itself, which

---

2. 'Paul and Union with Christ,' by Constantine R. Campbell; Zondervan, U.S.A., 2012; especially pp. 406-412.

captures the foundational idea of what it means for me to be in Christ and Christ in me. This is the faith union which is activated by the ministry of the Holy Spirit, but Campbell argues that this can appear to be a static state of affairs, rather than a dynamic living experience implying change and development.

So, to counteract this he draws attention to three other explanatory aspects, or terms, which help to augment our understanding of what this union is and how it operates. These he lists as participation, identification and incorporation. In the first, participation, the focus is on how we, as believers, share in the key events of the narrative of Christ's death and resurrection. A representative example is found in Ephesians 2:5-6. 'God made us alive together *with* Christ … and raised us up *with* him and seated us *with* him in the heavenly places *in* Christ Jesus.' Because we are united to Christ all that happened to Him is shared by those who are united to Him, as members of His body. This idea is developed in the further concept of identification with Christ, as we live in allegiance to His kingly rule and so are located in the realm of His lordship. 'There is neither Jew nor Greek, slave nor free, male nor female, for you are all one *in* Christ Jesus' (Gal. 3:28). And the third category of incorporation takes us further into this dimension of our membership of Christ's body. 'We, though many, are one body *in* Christ and individually members one of another' (Rom. 12:5). Or, again in Ephesians, Christ has created *in* himself one new man in place of the two so making peace … through the cross' (Eph. 2:15-16). And then, speaking of the household of God, built on Christ Jesus as the cornerstone, Paul writes '*in* whom the whole structure, being joined together, grows into a holy temple *in* the Lord. *In* him you also are being built together into a dwelling place for God by the Spirit' (2:20-21).

These additional dimensions of our union with Christ extend the scope and range of our understanding of this fundamental reality and help to rescue the concept from an overly individualistic, me-centred application, or from being viewed as an abstract theological proposition.

However, it is necessary to explore the classic location for Paul's unfolding of the impact which these realities of our union with Christ should have upon our everyday Christian lives, in Romans chapters 5 and 6. It may be a truism to say that the teaching of these chapters depends upon, and is built on, the first four chapters of the letter, but it is vital that as Bible teachers we acknowledge and follow the apostolic pattern. From the beginning of the letter Paul has been pursuing the theme that 'the one who by faith is righteous shall live' (Rom. 1:17 ESV footnote). But the natural state of every man, whether Gentile or Jew, is unrighteousness, which could never be remedied by the law. Since 'all have sinned and fall short of the glory of God' (the righteousness which God requires), the only way that anyone will be justified, accepted as righteous by God, is 'by his grace as a gift, through the redemption that is in Christ Jesus' (Rom. 3:23-24).

The laying of this foundation of our human inability to save ourselves from the righteous wrath of God against sin, along with the amazing grace of Christ's justifying work on the cross is the essential pre-requisite if we are to understand and embrace the totality of Christ's work in uniting us to Himself, by grace through faith. If there is no great awareness of our desperate state before God without Christ's saving intervention, there will be a shallowness of Christian experience reflected in a lack of gratitude and in half-hearted discipleship. 'He who is forgiven little loves little' (Luke 7:47). Part of our duty in teaching the Christian life is frequently to remind ourselves and our hearers of the enormity of our debt of sin and the consequent wonder of the justifying grace of God.

By the time we reach the mid-point of chapter 5, Paul is summarising what we have been taught so far about the grace of God in the gospel. 'For if while we were enemies we were reconciled to God by the death of his Son, much more, now that we are reconciled, shall we be saved by his life' (Rom. 5:10). This hinge verse launches us into a fuller exploration of what it means to be 'saved by his life', by pursuing the twin analogies of what it means to be 'in Adam' and 'in Christ'. In the second half of Romans 5 there are two dominant linguistic patterns which dictate the shape of the text.

The first of these is the structure 'if x, much more y', which shows the superiority of 'y', represented here by the grace of God in Jesus Christ. The 'if' is not problematic or questionable, it simply sets up the logic of the argument – if this was what it meant to be 'in Adam', see how 'much more' we have 'in Christ'. So, in verse 15, if many died through Adam's trespass. In verse 17, 'death reigned through that one man' and in verse 20, 'the law came in to increase the trespass'. But look at the 'much mores'. In verse 15, many died through Adam, 'much more have the grace of God and the free gift by the grace of that one man Jesus Christ abounded for many'. In verse 17, instead of death reigning, 'much more' grace, with its free gift of righteousness, will enable those who receive it to 'reign in life through the one man Jesus Christ'. In verse 20, if the law increased sin, 'grace abounded all the more'. The way the argument is structured is designed to elevate and glorify the grace of God in Christ and all the benefits which flow from Him to those who are united to Him, who are 'in Christ'.

The second pattern is 'just as ... so also', which introduces a similarity of operational mechanism, but with a radically different outcome, expressed in each comparison as 'righteousness'. Thus in verse 18, 'one trespass led to condemnation for all'. In the same way, 'one act of righteousness leads to justification and life for all'. In verse 19, 'the many were made sinners' by Adam's disobedience, exactly as by Christ's obedience 'the many will be made righteous'. Finally, in verse 21, 'as sin reigned in death, grace also might reign through righteousness leading to eternal life through Jesus Christ our Lord'. The purpose of expressing these realities in this pattern must be, at least partially, to help us better to understand the 'in Christ' teaching which is to follow in chapter 6. The 'in Adam' identification is something every reader can readily recognise from their personal experience. The problem of sin and condemnation is not foreign to us. We live under the reign of sin and death, from which there is no escape apart from the 'much more' grace of God. As we take that all-encompassing reality and transfer the same pattern to the realm of the free gift, we not only see the incomparable glories of the gospel, but we also begin to appreciate the radical change which occurs when we move from being 'in Adam' to being 'in Christ'. It is an inner change of domination, control, or life-principle, which brings the believer into a totally new world.

Teaching this material is an essential foundation for the development of a healthy life of faith and progressive godliness. It is all too easy to settle into the knowledge of sins forgiven through the death of Jesus, which is indeed the most wonderful good news we could ever hear, but there is so 'much more' to the grace of God revealed in the cross. Without this nourishing truth in our regular teaching we shall tend to assume that while we do have this gospel assurance it's up to us now to do the best we can. Of course, there is a human responsibility implicit in a right response to these truths, as we saw at the beginning of this chapter. We do have to seek to add to our faith and to work out our salvation. But the issue is how that can happen. If the 'much more' of grace and consequent righteousness is not central to our lives, we shall tend to slip into an incipient 'works religion', which is always the default position of our still sinful hearts. There is nothing so arid and miserable as a Christian seeking to climb little self-made ladders to find greater acceptance with God, or with others. The enemy then succeeds in diverting us from the source of our spiritual life in Christ Jesus, that life-giving relationship of love which is the essence of Christian faith, into a miserable backwater of religion based on achievement, or more likely, lack of it.

It is the same error that Jeremiah so powerfully exposed in the Jerusalem of his day. Through him, God warned, 'My people have committed two evils: they have forsaken me the fountain of living water, and hewed out cisterns for themselves, broken cisterns that can hold no water'

(Jer. 2:13). You only go back to digging for water, to the old life 'in Adam', when you forsake your dependence on the life-giving water of Christ. Remember His promise. 'Whoever drinks of the water that I will give him will never be thirsty forever. The water that I will give him will become in him a spring of water welling up to eternal life' (John 4:14).

There are two other major benefits which result from ensuring that these truths are taught consistently to our people. The first concerns the peace and security of the believer. There are so many anxious and stressed-out brothers and sisters in our churches, who live in constant insecurity and apprehension of difficulties and disasters. Not only are they effectively paralysed by this, but the contagion can very easily spread through the whole congregation and is particularly virulent in families, where growing children begin to think that what they hear in church has minimal influence on life at home. To understand and <u>really</u> believe that there is nothing in life for which God's grace is not 'much more' than adequate will always deepen our relationship as we bring to Him all the detailed challenges of life. We learn in practice that 'my God will supply every need of yours according to his riches in glory in Christ Jesus' (Phil. 4:19).

The other great benefit is to our evangelism. To return to the metaphor of the fountain of living waters, when Jesus invited anyone who was thirsty to come to Him and drink, He promised, 'Whoever believes in me, as the Scripture has said, "Out of his heart (inner being) will flow rivers of living water!"' (John 7:37-38). John tells us that He said this about the Spirit, but His work is of course the product of our being 'in Christ'. Evangelism is the overflow of the life-style of grace. When we drink deeply of Jesus, living in communion with Him, 'in Christ', His life in us will inevitably flow out to others. It doesn't have to be pumped up; it will overflow. There is a spiritual power of life in Christ received by faith which cannot be contained, but overflows, like a flood, bringing life to others. We need to learn that the dynamic for evangelism is the life of Christ within and not simply training in what can often seem a mechanistic, non-relational process.

What makes the world thirsty is when they see poverty-stricken children of Adam adopted into the family of the living God, united indissolubly to His Son, by grace through faith, and rejoicing in newness of life in Him. We are very privileged to have so many fine aids to evangelism in our generation, along with excellent training courses, but while they can equip they do not in themselves motivate or energise. What is needed most is for us, as believers, to be drinking deeply of Jesus, believing in Him, trusting Him and appropriating His limitless grace through our union with Him, so that overflow becomes the norm. That is why the teaching ministry and its careful exposition of Biblical truth is so vital for the health and welfare of the church and for her outreach to the world.

We need now to examine Romans 6, both because it is a key passage for the exposition of the Christian's union with Christ and also because it highlights essential truths which it is important to ensure are being given due emphasis through-out our teaching ministries. Verse 1 is dealing with a real practical and pastoral problem. 'Are we to continue in sin that grace may abound?' This is precisely what we are tempted to do if we simply rejoice in the abundance of God's grace without recognising its corollary that grace must reign through righteousness. If one of the perils of misunderstanding, or not being taught, these truths is the incipient slide into works religion and even legalism, the other equal and opposite danger is antinomianism. Again its influence is often hidden and subtle, but it surfaces every time confession of sin is reduced to simply 'saying sorry to God', rather than with a 'humble, lowly, penitent and obedient heart' as the Book of Common Prayer exhorts. This focuses one of the prevalent weaknesses of much contemporary evangelicalism. We fail to identify sin as sin and so we fail truly to repent. We actually begin to imagine that God's grace is so indulgent that He is complicit with our redefinition of our favourite sins as our little weaknesses or peccadilloes.

Soon we begin to devalue the amazing grace of God in the cross of Christ and to slide into an easy-come, easy-go version of Christianity, which neither changes the individual nor challenges the world. No wonder Paul's horrified response is 'By no means!' That is not what we have been saved for.

His rejoinder, in verse 2, is 'we died to sin' and this essential truth is repeated several times in the chapter. 'Our old self was crucified with him' (v. 6). 'We have died with Christ' (v. 8). The implication is clear, 'So you must consider yourselves dead to sin ...' (v. 11). They are all tenses of completed action in the past. They relate to a death that has already happened. Just as the end of chapter 5 taught us that 'sin reigned in death' (v. 21), so chapter 6 expresses a decisive end to that state of affairs. The implications are clearly spelt out – 'no longer enslaved

to sin' (v. 6), 'set free from sin' (v. 7), 'sin will have no
dominion over you' (v. 14). Here again it is easy to fall
into the traps of moralism ('you could be free if you just
follow these rules') or perfectionism ('you will be free if
you achieve these standards') but the text says that it is
an accomplished fact. We are no longer in Adam. We
have crossed the border. We are in Christ and from a
theological standpoint dual citizenship is impossible.

'We died with Christ' (v. 8) is explained in several ways
in the course of these verses. Verse 3 speaks about being
'baptized into his death' and verse 4 about being 'buried
with him'. Verse 5 says 'we have been united with him in
a death like his', explained in verse 6 as 'our old self was
crucified with him in order that the body of sin (the old
"in Adam" way of living) might be brought to nothing.'
Commenting on this verse, John Stott notes, 'What was
crucified with Christ was not a part of us called my old
nature, but the whole of us as we were in our pre-conversion
state'.[3] What happened actually and with lasting potential
when Christ died is then realised personally when we
repent and believe the gospel. Hence there is the link to
baptism in verses 3-4, as the beginning of our Christian
experience. Baptism is the outward, physical sign of the
inward transforming grace, by which we were transferred
from life 'in Adam' to life 'in Christ'.

Our union with Christ in His death means that through
faith all the benefits of the atonement have become ours.
We are justified; we have peace with God; we have obtained
access into God's grace; we rejoice in hope of God's glory

---

3. 'The Message of Romans,' by John R. W. Stott; IVP, Leicester, 1994;
   p. 176.

(Rom. 5:1-2). Our union with Christ in His burial confirms our release from sin's dominion. Our union with Christ in His resurrection means that 'death no longer has dominion over him' or over us (v. 9) so that 'we too might walk in newness of life' (v. 4). The Christ to whom we are united and in whom we live is the crucified and risen Lord.

It is important to remember that the practical, trans-formational purpose of these great theological realities is uppermost in Paul's thinking here, as verses 6-7 make clear. The structure of verse 6 is important. 'We know ... in order that.' The practical application is the outcome of the spiritual knowledge. The teaching has to come first, but its purpose is not just enlightenment but a life-changing dynamic. This is what enables our old sin-dominated, 'in Adam' way of life, to be 'brought to nothing'. Paraphrases of this verb include to be reduced to inactivity, to be made of no effect, nullified, or done away with. This is why it is so important to teach the implications as well as the means of justification. As the Reformers insisted, every believer in Christ is both justified and at the same time a sinner still. John Stott makes the point with his customary clarity and succinctness when he comments, 'We are not to pretend that our old nature has died, when we know perfectly well it has not. Instead we realize and remember that our former self did die with Christ, thus putting an end to its career'.[4] It is that realizing and remembering which Paul is referencing when in verse 11 he tells us that we must 'consider yourselves dead to sin and alive to God in Christ Jesus'. 'In Christ' our old pre-Christian life style has been

---

4. op. cit., p. 179.

deprived of its controlling power and rule. The tyranny has been defeated and so we are no longer enslaved to sin.

But what does this look like in everyday life? The crucifixion was followed by the resurrection and the two cannot be separated. 'Now if we have died with Christ, we believe we will also live with him' (v. 8). This is not, however, simply to be interpreted as referring to the 'not yet' of the eternal kingdom in its consummation. That kingdom has already broken into time and space history and is already operative in our 'now' experience as justified sinners. In verses 9-10 Paul connects the pattern of the death and resurrection of Christ to our own discipleship, since we are in union with Him. It starts with a once-for-all event, the crucifixion, by which the old has gone and continues with the new eternal life, begun by Christ's resurrection, which is lived in a totally new realm of experience. 'The life he lives he lives to God' and so do we if we are 'in Christ' (v. 10).

The first eleven verses of the chapter are the foundational teaching of the truth, before the specific application is made in verses 12-13. Even verse 11 must not be seen as an exhortation for us to make something happen, but to reckon that because it has already happened, in the cross and resurrection, all these benefits of grace are available now to us. It is a given principle of apostolic teaching that only after the indicatives have been expounded can the imperatives be applied. We would do well always to follow this pattern in our own teaching. The sort of careful analysis we have sketched here, although only in outline, pays careful attention to the surface structure and composition of the paragraph, because exegesis of this sort is what will give logical coherence and persuasive strength to the exposition and therefore also to its application.

At verse 12, 'therefore' finally reaches the direct application of the passage. It comes in three verses (12-14), in the form of two negatives, two positives and one closing assurance. Twice we are told 'Do not'. In fact, it is striking that in verse 12 the reader is directly addressed ('you') for the first time in the epistle. Perhaps Paul begins with the negative because it is often the means by which the positive becomes clearer and more illuminating. Certainly it is a good teaching method from which we can learn. It also establishes the understanding that the reader has a responsible personal part to play in entering into this newness of life in Christ. There are two things the Christian must not do. Do not let sin reign (v. 12) and do not present your members to sin (v. 13). The body is clearly the conflict area where Paul pictures sin as trying to regain its authority, by persuading us to use our appetites and functions for evil passions or desires, as 'instruments for unrighteousness'.

We need to be clear that Paul never says that sin is dead to us, but that we died to sin. He reminds us in verse 12 that our bodies are mortal (the wages of sin) as though to underline that the virus is always there in the body, until it is transformed into the likeness of Christ's glorious body at the last day (Phil. 3:21). Until then the only way to carry out the 'do not' application is by carrying out the positives of verse 13 – 'present yourselves to God … and your members as instruments for righteousness'. That is our responsibility. Not only our physical faculties, but also our minds, imaginations, wills and emotions are all to be

consciously placed at God's disposal. Note the order. First
we are to present ourselves and then our members. First
the heart, the control-centre of the personality, what we
might call 'the real you' belongs to God who has brought us
from death to life and then all the constituent ingredients
of our lives in this world are to be put into His hands. As
Romans 12:1 will teach us, this is 'your spiritual worship'.

The wonderful promise with which the section ends
in verse 14 has within it two key linking words—'for' and
'since'. They could both be rendered 'because'—one is the
result and the other the reason. Notice that there is no
'then' in the verse. He does not say 'for then (if you do this)
sin will not reign'. It is not an exhortation or command; it
is a promise. This is the great purpose of God's saving work
in Christ and it will be an eternal reality, so you can live
that way now. Sin is no longer your tyrant, nor ever will be.
A change of rule has taken place. We are no longer 'under
law' ('do this and you will live') which could only bring the
knowledge of sin (3:20) and the consequent wrath of God
(4:15). We are 'under grace'. We live in a union of love with
our gracious rescuer, who is risen in power and shares His
eternal life with us here and now. We have a new dynamic
at work within us, changing us from the inside out. We
have not only open access to God, but personal fellowship
with Him in a new relationship of love, joy and peace. We
have a new destination and certainty of final full salvation
in glory for ever. We have a new set of opportunities and
responsibilities in the love and service of our king. We can
live a life of progressive holiness, as we appropriate by faith
all the benefits of our union with Christ, in and through
His death and resurrection. This is a wonderful conclusion

to Paul's argument in this section and we need to teach it with such conviction and enthusiasm as to stir, excite and motivate our hearers with a deepening awareness of the huge privileges which belong to those who are 'in Christ'.

Do you see how this healthy corrective changes so much of our contemporary thinking about the Christian life? It moves us away from a predominantly subjective focus on me and my needs. Certainly, the church sometimes has to function as a field hospital to treat and care for wounded soldiers injured in the battle. But it is not designed to be a clinic for spiritual hypochondriacs. Too many Christians seem to have succumbed to accepting themselves as always being spiritually weak and sickly. I am not speaking about physical or psychological needs or illnesses here, which sadly will always be some part of our experience living in a fallen world. What I mean is that the church is not intended to become a centre of unhealthy introspection, with a focus on what we don't have, or what we think we cannot do or become. We are not to become addicted to a problem-centred approach, either to our own lives, or those around us. We need to lift our vision to see who we truly are 'in Christ' and all the blessings of our union with Him. Above all we need to fix our eyes on Jesus and cultivate our relationship with Him.

It is the Bible teacher's responsibility to encourage this through consistent expository ministry of the Scriptures. Our horizons are generally far too limited. We need to realise that in union with Christ God has caught us up in the greatest and most significant narrative in the universe. He has enlisted us in a cause immeasurably greater than our little selves and our transient lives which are like 'a mist that appears for a little time and then vanishes' (James 4:14). He has made us citizens of His eternal kingdom and calls us to present ourselves and our members as instruments of righteousness, to serve our Lord with every aspect of our being. This is our responsibility—our response to His ability—for as long as we are in this world.

12.

Preaching that develops maturity

'Brothers, do not be children in your thinking. Be infants in evil, but in your thinking be mature' (1 Cor. 14:20). In context, the apostle Paul is dealing with the use and abuse of the gift of tongues in the church at Corinth, but the principle he underlines here has relevance across the whole spectrum of church life and ministry. Already in 1 Corinthians 3:1 Paul has chided them, 'But I, brothers, could not address you as spiritual people, but as people of the flesh, as infants in Christ.' Clearly, spiritual immaturity is associated with being governed still by the flesh and all that it is attracted to. It is evidenced every time we turn back to our pre-Christian way of living, to the values, priorities and deceptive promises of a world at enmity with God. The Corinthians were excited by the spectacular externals of the faith and the same problem is still with us. Like children, we are naturally attracted all too easily to the novel and the glitzy, because we would rather walk by sight than by faith and we would rather feel good than think deeply. This means that it is one of the greatest and most persistent challenges in ministry to

develop in ourselves and our hearers a truly Biblical, and
therefore Christ-like, mind-set.

It has been our recurring theme throughout these chapters
that the health and effectiveness of both our individual
Christian lives and our corporate church communities
are directly dependent on the ministry of God's word.
Preaching and teaching the Bible is the indispensable core
of all Christian ministry. And this is because any ministry
deserving the title 'Christian' is derived from Christ and
exercised under His authority, which means according to
His declared priorities. Jesus Himself clearly stated them,
with regard to His own earthly ministry. 'I do nothing on my
own authority, but speak just as the Father taught me ... for I
always do the things that are pleasing to him' (John 8:28-29).
It was the Father's word which was the content of Jesus'
ministry and passing on that word was what brought the
Father pleasure. This is the same ministry to which the risen
Lord commissioned His disciples, in the power of the Holy
Spirit. 'As the Father has sent me, even so I am sending you'
(John 20:21-22). Any claim to authentic Christian ministry
must therefore be evaluated by the same priorities. It can be
achieved by a variety of means, but primary to them all is the
accurate and faithful transmission of God's revealed truth
to the mind, heart and will of the believer, so as to develop
a whole-person and whole life-style maturity. Whether
in personal Bible reading or the teaching ministry of the
church, through preaching, teaching and study-groups,
whether in evangelism or edification, the same priority must
always be central.

Expository preaching will therefore, by its very nature,
be educational, since God's purpose is to produce a people

whose thinking is spiritually mature. It should instruct the minds of the hearers, so that the truth of God's revelation is grasped and understood. It should apply that truth to the heart, the Biblical control-centre of the personality, so that its life-transforming message can be both received and embraced. It should challenge the will, so that the impression made on mind and heart is translated into life-changing action, through the enabling of the Holy Spirit. And this process of whole person 'education' is necessary to produce the maturity which is the goal of every Bible preacher, as it was of the apostles (Col. 1:28).

However, there is a danger that when we think of 'maturity' we tend to define and then assess it by criteria which owe more to our cultural values in the contemporary world and church than to the Scriptures. When individuals are described as 'keen' Christians, that assessment is often made on the basis of visible activities. While that is a natural way to respond, we need to remember that 'the Lord sees not as man sees: man looks on the outward appearance, but the Lord looks on the heart' (1 Sam. 16:7). Only He can discern its thoughts and intentions. For example, in some churches today the measuring-stick for maturity is in regard to the work of evangelism. Church leaders tend to most value those who are 'bringers', whose activity is gathering others in. Of course, there is ample support for this in the great commission of Matthew 28:19-20, where making disciples is key, though it should be noticed that equally important in the verse is teaching all that Jesus commanded.

The widespread ignorance of the gospel across the western world today is a huge challenge and God's people naturally long to see the spread of the good news of God's saving power. But if the mark of Christian growth is restricted to evangelistic activity, there are two likely consequences, which are often overlooked. Firstly, the more reserved and reflective members of the congregation can come to see themselves as undervalued and even insignificant because they are not naturally easy communicators and have, in their eyes, only a record of failure in leading others to Christ. They may feel guilty about this, or just resistant, but either way they pick up the signal that they are not quite what is wanted, classified as second-class disciples. Not only does this work against the unity of the body, where the different gifts and functions of each of the members are needed for the whole body to function properly and upbuild itself in love, but it also devalues the invisible, hidden evidences of love for Christ, in terms of private prayer, unsung works of love, low-profile pastoral support for the weak and vulnerable – none of which will ever hit the headlines.

Secondly, the emphasis on activity as the measure of maturity is liable to divert attention away from devotion to the Lord Jesus into building 'our church'. Once again, of course, the two are not incompatible; actually, they belong together. But it is all too easy for the church to replace Christ, as the centre of our spiritual lives and love, with itself. Remember how the Ephesian church is told by the risen Lord that while they are to be commended for their works, toil and patient endurance, yet they have abandoned the love they had at first (Rev. 2:2-4). Congregations are shaped in how they think about God and how they read and apply Scripture, not only by the teaching they receive, but by the modelling they see in their teachers. It is a good exercise to ask ourselves whether our primary devotion is to building a spiritual enterprise called 'our church', or whether our activity is the overflow of the living waters that comes from drinking deeply of Christ and sustains our whole existence spiritually.

The Bible's definition of 'maturity' is likeness to Christ, which means loving God with every aspect of our being, whether or not it is expressed in any one particular way, which we may prioritise. It means loving my neighbour as myself. It involves caring about God's truth and caring with compassion for the lost. Its concern is for character over activity. All this flows out of a deepening knowledge of God, communion with Him and heart-love for Him. That is the expression of faith, which can only be produced as the Word of God impacts mind, heart and will, our thoughts, decision-making and emotions, through the gracious work of the Holy Spirit. His fruit, the evidence of maturity, is 'love, joy, peace, patience, kindness, goodness, faithfulness, gentleness and self-control' (Gal. 5:22-23). Perhaps one of the reasons why our preaching is less effective in developing spiritual maturity than we would like it to be might lie here. Could it be that we concentrate too much and too soon on the practical application of the Bible to all the activities we want our hearers to undertake, at the expense of feeding their minds and warming their hearts with an increasing awareness of the majesty and glory of the God who is truth? So, what can the Scriptures themselves teach us about how to cultivate increasingly mature Christians thinking and living?

The foundational understanding is that the new mind is created in the individual believer by God Himself, as a consequence of the new birth. When Paul declares that 'if anyone is in Christ, he is a new creation' (2 Cor. 5:17), he must at least be affirming that the new spiritual life within will have its impact in transforming the believer's whole mind-set. As with any organism, what has been created will need to grow and develop, but the fundamental change has already happened. This means that the Bible teacher can, and should, appeal to the 'good work' which God has already begun (Phil. 1:6), so that as believers we are positively depending on, and co-operating with, the ongoing work of the Spirit. Although we may consider that the thinking process is in itself neutral, there is always some object or direction to which our thoughts are moving, which will determine our orientation, priorities and preferences and which will then shape our words and actions. In all of this the new mind has a new direction, as Paul explains in Romans 8:5-6. 'For those who live according to the flesh set their minds on the things of the flesh, but those who live according to the Spirit set their minds on the things of the Spirit. For to set the mind on the flesh is death, but to set the mind on the Spirit is life and peace.' The translation 'set the mind on' implies a definite mental decision that occurs when we are born again and which causes a radical transformation of thinking, which as it develops crystallizes into a new 'mind set'. The issue for the Christian in all such decision-making is whether this is to be the way of the flesh (our sinful nature) or of the Spirit.

Commenting on the Romans 8 verses, J. Goetzmann writes, 'This passage makes it abundantly clear that the way one thinks is intimately related to the way one lives, whether in Christ, in the Spirit and by faith, or alternatively in the flesh, in sin and in spiritual death. A man's thinking and striving cannot be seen in isolation from the overall direction of his life; the latter will be reflected in the aims which he sets himself'.[1] Similarly, in 1 Corinthians 2 where Paul affirms that 'we have the mind of Christ' (v. 16), he is concerned to stress that this does not mean that we are able to understand God's mind, or think as He thinks, because 'no one comprehends the thoughts of God except the Spirit of God' (v. 11). Moreover, speaking of the 'secret and hidden wisdom of God' (v. 7) he affirms that 'these things God has revealed to us through the Spirit' (v. 10), which is the consequence of the new birth. For 'we have received not the spirit of the world, but the Spirit who is from God, that we might understand the things freely given us by God' (v. 12).

Developing the new, spiritual mind-set is therefore the most natural expected outcome of the new birth. It is a favourite theme of Paul's writings as we saw earlier. In Ephesians 4:20, he describes conversion as 'learning Christ', which is followed by the exhortation to put off your old self and put on the new, 'created after the likeness of God in true righteousness and holiness' (vv. 22-24). Most significant, however, is that this will happen as his readers are 'renewed in the spirit of your minds' (v. 23), and it is this new thinking which is then worked out in the detailed examples of Christian living—walking in love (5:2), in light (5:8) and in wisdom (5:15)—which make up the rest of the letter. It is the same pattern in Colossians 3:2, where the exhortation is, 'Set your minds on things that are above,

---

1. J. Goetzmann, article on 'Mind' in 'The New International Dictionary of New Testament Theology, Volume 2'; Paternoster Press, Exeter 1976; pp. 616-620.

not on things that are on earth'. And recognising that the new mind-set dictates a new life-style, the rest of this letter similarly focuses on a whole raft of practical applications (see 3:5-4:6).

This emphasis reminds us that Christian living depends on a mind that is constantly being refreshed and re-filled with the knowledge of God and His ways. In the title of J. I. Packer's famous book, the Christian life is about 'knowing God', not merely knowing about Him. The mind works on knowledge, but in Scripture that knowledge is personal and relational, not merely academic or theoretical. Modern education tends to emphasise analytical skills and theoretical experimentation, which certainly have their use, much as a text book of systematic theology has its use, but the acquisition of such tools does not at all guarantee the personal knowledge of the only true God and Jesus Christ whom He sent, which is eternal life (John 17:3). However, the reaction to the sort of head knowledge that 'puffs up' (1 Cor. 8:1) is not to swing to the opposite pole, where the mind is governed by the emotions or feelings. Often when Paul is correcting wrong beliefs, attitudes or conduct he resorts to the formula, 'Do you not know ...?' Christians are to be people whose minds are equipped with that true knowledge, which comes from God's revelation in Scripture. This was the ministry of the risen Lord to His confused disciples after His resurrection. 'Then he opened their minds to understand the Scriptures' (Luke 24:45). That is the highest use of the Christian mind, because it is then engaging with ultimate truth, given in the divine self-revelation, rather than simply weighing and assessing human perceptions.

This is such an important principle of Christian growth to maturity because it liberates us from the tyranny of subjective feelings and from the often dead-end of 'feeling led'. Sadly, sincere believers can frequently be led astray if instead of giving their minds to God's truth in Scripture they devote their mental energies towards their own desires and imaginations, in the hope that the 'inner voice' may actually be from God.

But what about the many areas of life where the choices we have to make are not directly governed by specific Biblical commandments, which are the revelation of God's unchanging character and which are given to be obeyed?

'For this is the love of God, that we keep his commandments. And his commandments are not burdensome' (1 John 5:3). But there are many areas of life where the decision is not between right and wrong, good and evil, but between wisdom and folly. These require a maturity of Biblical thinking in order to come to Christian conclusions. The Bible's way is not to provide a system or impersonal code to be applied automatically to every issue. There is no Biblical blue-print for every situation of life, but there are principles, reflecting the character of the God who has revealed them, which have to be recognised and applied to the specifics of each context. That is because we are called to walk by faith and not by sight and because Christian maturity is the process of becoming increasingly dependent on the grace of God.

We might sum up these important issues of developing our Christian thinking or mind-set in this chapter by the one word, 'wisdom'. This is a major ingredient of the whole revelation of Scripture, but one that is frequently under-played in our teaching programmes. Yet Old Testament 'wisdom' is an important genre, exhibited not only in whole books, such as Job, Proverbs and Ecclesiastes, but also as a significant strand of instruction and reflection in many psalms and prophetic oracles. Indeed, it has been suggested that the wise person (sometimes called the sage) is almost as distinct a category in Israelite society as the prophet, priest or king. Solomon is, of course, the supreme example of the wise king, since 'God gave him wisdom and understanding beyond measure and breadth of mind like the sand on the seashore' (1 Kings 4:29ff). So when Jesus declared Himself to be 'something greater than Solomon' as He taught the crowds (Matt. 12:42), He was indicating that not only had He come to fulfil the offices of prophet, priest and king, but also that of the wise man, as He was in Himself the personification of divine wisdom.

The purpose of wisdom writers is essentially applicatory. Biblical wisdom relates the revelational truth of the historical narratives, the law and the prophets to the experience of living life in the real world in both its fallenness and its immense potential. In that sense, the sinless earthly life of Jesus is the perfect embodiment of wisdom and sets the example for His followers to seek to emulate. Much of His teaching by parables and aphorisms is clearly rooted in the wisdom tradition. But the emphasis throughout the Bible is not that wisdom is the fruit of groping our way through life and hopefully acquiring positive experience by a process of trial and error. That is worldly 'wisdom', which God has declared to be empty, because it can never produce the knowledge of God (1 Cor. 1:20-21). Such knowledge is only by God's self-revelation and so the fundamental conviction about Biblical wisdom is that it is God's gift (Prov. 2:6). And this explains why Paul can remind the Christians in Corinth that '(God) is the source of your life in Christ Jesus, whom God made our wisdom and our righteousness and sanctification and redemption' (1 Cor. 1:30). They are all the gracious gifts of God.

This is hugely encouraging to us, as we engage in the task of growing in wisdom personally, as well as helping those we serve to live increasingly wisely in God's world, by God's Spirit. What we all need is divine help in learning through His self-revelation in Scripture, so that we can understand and apply its teaching to the constantly changing range of challenges with which life in our contemporary world provides us. That is precisely the function of God's gift of wisdom.

So, let us teach and rejoice in the fact that true wisdom is the gift of God's inexhaustible grace, which means that it will always find its focus and content in God's inexpressible gift of His beloved Son (2 Cor. 9:15). He is our wisdom. The apostle Paul links the riches of God's lavish grace to the wisdom and insight given to His people through the unfolding of His eternal purposes, in the gospel (Eph. 1:8-9). Because wisdom is God's gift, he asks the Father of glory to give the Ephesians 'a spirit of wisdom and of revelation in the knowledge of Him (Christ)' (Eph. 1:17). Similarly, he tells the Colossians that he constantly prays for them to be filled with the knowledge of God's will, 'in all spiritual wisdom and understanding' (Col. 1:9). But immediately that is linked to the practical applicatory nature of true spiritual wisdom to everyday life, 'so as to walk in a manner

worthy of the Lord, fully pleasing to him, bearing fruit in
every good work and increasing in the knowledge of God'
(Col. 1:10). In both letters there is a behavioural focus on
the outcome of God's gift of wisdom (Eph. 5:15, Col 4:5),
because the believer's life of wisdom is a persuasive proof
of the revolutionary dynamic of the gospel, not least to the
hostile spiritual powers. The present stage of God's eternal
purposes, realised in Christ, and to be fully revealed in the
fulness of time when all creation will be under His feet,
is that 'through the church the manifold wisdom of God
might now be made known to the rulers and authorities
in the heavenly places' (Eph. 3:10). Only in Christ could
believing Jews and Gentiles live in harmony and love as one
new creation, because in Christ alone 'are hidden all the
treasures of wisdom and knowledge' (Col. 2:3).

The letter of James adds a final encouraging perspective
to this pursuit of wisdom, for there is a progression built in to
our experience of God's gracious gift. If at times we may feel
that although wisdom is the gift of God, we are lacking in
that department, then James points us to the remedy. 'If any
of you lacks wisdom, let him ask God, who gives generously
to all without reproach, and it will be given him' (James 1:5).
Those words 'without reproach' are surely intended as a great
incentive to prayer. God knows our foolishness. He wants us
to receive His wisdom, but He also wants us to ask Him for
it. And how shall we know that we have indeed received it?
'By his good conduct let him show his works in the meekness
of wisdom' (James 3:13), for 'the wisdom from above is first
pure, then peaceable, gentle, open to reason, full of mercy
and good fruits, impartial and sincere' (James 3:17). Here is
a picture of the wise, and therefore godly believer, of which

the Lord Jesus is the only perfect example; but we are called to follow in His steps. If we desire these characteristics to be exemplified in our own lives and in our churches, then we need to preach the wisdom literature of both testaments, so that in our thinking and consequent actions we are growing towards maturity.

Such growth will never go unchallenged and is by no means automatic. After the first eleven chapters of Paul's magnificent exposition of the gospel, in his letter to the Romans, his immediate application in chapter 12 is that the spiritual response of worship is to present one's body as a living sacrifice and also to be transformed by the renewal of one's mind. But in between, there is the stark warning, 'Do not be conformed to this world' (Rom. 12:1-2) or as one paraphrase has put it, 'Don't let the world squeeze you into its mould.' The pressure is always there. The world in which we live is not neutral. 'The whole world lies in the power of the evil one' (1 John 5:19), and it will do all that it can to produce conformity to its norms and systems in the life of any unwary believer. The battleground is clearly every Christian's mind, but the proof of developing godliness is not in terms of theoretical knowledge, but in its translation into life-style. It is striking that the next verse in Romans 12 reads, 'For by the grace given to me I say to everyone among you not to think of himself more highly than he ought to think, but to think with sober judgment' (v. 3). This is the fruit of the grace of the gospel and is applicable to us all ('everyone'), 'each according to the measure of faith that God has assigned' (v. 3b). Faith is itself God's gift, as are all the abilities and endowments which each believer has. There can be no room for pride and self-conceit in such a context because what we are is entirely the product of God's grace. No maturing Christian can have an inflated view of their own importance when this 'knowledge' is in control. The world is proud of its knowledge and achievements and boasting of who one is and what one has is endemic to its culture. 'But not so with you', Jesus told His disciples. 'Rather, let the greatest among you become as the youngest, and the leader as one who serves. For who is the greater, one who reclines at table or one who serves? Is it not the one who reclines at table? But I am among you as the one who serves' (Luke 22:25-27).

One of the greatest challenges for those of us who are pastors and teachers is to model to the believers the humility of Christ, not in a self-conscious way, but as the natural and genuine outworking of the mind of Christ, both in what we say and do and especially in how we say and do it. The classic passage is, of course, the great 'parabola' of Philippians 2:5-11, which traces the downward steps of the Lord Jesus as He laid aside His glory, took the form of a servant and humbled Himself even to the point of death on a cross. What then follows, as a consequence, is His exaltation to glory and rule over the whole of creation. Such service is unique to the Lord Jesus, but it is striking that Paul precedes his exposition of Christ's ministry with the exhortation to the church, 'Have this mind among yourselves, which is yours in Christ Jesus' (or ESV footnote, 'which was also in Christ Jesus'). He traces the very work of salvation to the mind-set of Christ—He accomplished His work because He thought this way—and so immediately before and after the great Christological passage it is clear that the apostle is using the person and work of Christ to inculcate in His followers the same mind-set, the same values. Here is the pattern of Christ's mind-set related to the thinking of His followers, so as to shape and govern our life-style as it did His, in sacrificial service.

Twice, in Philippians 2:2, Paul appeals to the Philippian church to be 'of the same mind ... being in full accord and of one mind', which is the mind of Christ. Verses 3-4 underline how very practical and down-to-earth this is. It means no rivalry or conceit, in humility counting others more significant than oneself, looking not only to one's own interests but also to the interests of others. This is the mind-set of Christ-like maturity. Similarly in verses 14-15, Paul exhorts his readers to 'do all things without grumbling or questioning, that you may be blameless and innocent, children of God without blemish in the midst of a crooked and twisted generation ...' Only the mind of Christ can produce a life-style like His, but it is a necessary authentication of the transforming power of the Lord of the gospel, if we are to be able to shine 'as lights in the world'. If the darkness around so often seems to engulf the church in the world, could it be because our life-style and our thinking are not distinctly Christ-like enough to have any illuminating power?

Clearly the remedy for all such deficiencies must lie in the Scriptures, 'breathed out by God and profitable for teaching, for reproof, for correction, and for training in righteousness, that the man of God may be competent, equipped for every good work' (2 Tim. 3:16-17). The primary reference here is to the pastor-teacher as 'the man of God', whose ministry in preaching the Word is to 'reprove, rebuke and exhort, with complete patience and teaching' (4:2). So the teaching ministry holds the key to the church becoming fit for purpose in its divine calling, to hold out the Word of life to the dying world. At the end of Paul's life, he is deeply aware of the developing denial of the power of the gospel within the church through compromise with the world. 'For people will be lovers of self, lovers of money ... lovers of pleasure rather than lovers of God, having the appearance of godliness but denying its power' (2 Tim. 3:2-5). That is why his exhortation to Timothy is to 'preach the Word'. But if compromise is a fatal reaction to the pressures of the world to squeeze the church into its mould, withdrawal into a pious ghetto is equally destructive and disastrous. In his first letter to Timothy, Paul identifies the danger of teaching which encourages Christians so to deny the created order that they retreat into a 'bubble' of separatism, seeking to cultivate a sort of unreal 'spirituality', as though ordinary life had no real or lasting significance. His denunciation is totally uncompromising.

But if there is to be no division between the sacred and the secular in our thinking and experience, because our lives are to be a unified whole under Christ's lordship, there is clearly a great difference and division between the kingdom of this world and the kingdom of heaven. This is not to be construed as a total separation, since in Christ the kingdom of heaven has already invaded our world of time and space with all the unmistakable signs already of its ultimate consummation and victory in eternity. However, because of the fall and the continuance of human rebellion in rejecting God's testimony and denying His deity, there is an ongoing cosmic warfare in which every believer is involved, not against flesh and blood, but 'against the rulers, against the authorities, against the cosmic power over this present darkness, against the spiritual forces of evil in the heavenly places' (Eph. 6:12). It is an important part of our teaching ministry to keep underlining the reality and inevitability of this conflict. No progress is made towards godly maturity without opposition and challenges all along the way. But it is equally important to recognise this from a Biblically positive perspective. All too often the conflict can make us feel that we are always on the back foot, defensive, or even pessimistic and defeatist. Not so, with the New Testament writers!

Perhaps the major difference between the apostles and ourselves can best be understood in terms of perspective. In our contemporary culture the emphasis is very much on the present and the cultivation of personal fulfilment. For many, in the western world, the present is far more comfortable and pleasant than for any previous generations, which breeds the illusion that it has long-term stability and is under our control, until an emergency like the Covid-19 virus begins to unsettle things. As we are all affected by this prevailing ethos far more than we are usually prepared to admit, it is not surprising that we want to make our spiritual lives as comfortable and fulfilling as possible. We tend to regard the future, whether in this life or beyond it, as not having much impact on the way we live now until some emergency occurs that forces us to re-think. But the apostles seem to have lived by a different mind-set, a different priority of values.

In 2 Corinthians 4:1 and 16 Paul twice gives testimony
that we (the apostolic messengers) 'do not lose heart'.
But the context makes clear to us why he might have had
every reason to, we might think. He writes, 'For this slight
momentary affliction is preparing for us an eternal weight
of glory beyond all comparison' (2 Cor. 4:17). His present
experience is 'affliction' and two chapters later he tells
us what that involved – 'hardships, calamities, beatings,
imprisonments, riots, labours, sleepless nights, hunger'
(2 Cor. 6:4-5). There is an even more detailed catalogue of
what the sufferings of Paul's present life involved still later
in the letter (see 2 Cor. 11:23-28). Why did he not lose
heart? Because his perspective is that these afflictions are
only slight and momentary, when compared to the eternal
weight of glory, the unseen realities and rewards of the
heavenly, eternal kingdom. The present is preparing the
Christian for the future. The verb is emphatic and active –
it works out and achieves an effect. The suffering is actually
changing the sufferer as his focus is changed to become
oriented towards the eternal future. As verse 18 concludes,
'We look not to the things that are seen (transient) but to
the things that are unseen (eternal).'

The question for us is whether our ministry is cultivating
a robust mind-set which enables the contemporary believer
who is suffering trials, tribulations and afflictions, as
we all do in this fallen world, not to lose heart. Do we
understand and teach the practical wisdom of the New
Testament, that trials have an active and necessary role,
under God, in promoting spiritual maturity? A good test
might be to ask what our reaction is to a verse like James
1:2, 'Count it all joy, my brothers, when you meet trials

of various kinds.' Is that just pious escapism, by denial? Or a Stoical, masochistic streak that imagines the more it hurts the better we shall be for it? Neither is valid in the light of what follows, 'for you know that the testing of your faith produces steadfastness ... that you may be perfect and complete, lacking in nothing' (v. 3-4). There is the same verb we saw in 2 Corinthians 4:17. The trials produce; they work out an effect, which is hugely beneficial to our Christian growth to maturity. They develop faithful endurance.

Paul has the same thought in Romans 5:3-5 where his attitude to suffering is one of rejoicing, 'knowing that suffering produces endurance, and endurance produces character, and character produces hope and hope does not put us to shame ...' Again it is the same verb 'produce' which links together these ingredients in the chain of maturity. Moreover, Peter reiterates the point in his first letter when he speaks about rejoicing in the power of God which guards His people through faith 'for a salvation ready to be revealed in the last time'. His eyes are firmly fixed on the future glory, although he realises that for his readers 'now, for a little while, if necessary, you have been grieved by various trials'. But why would they be 'necessary'? The next verse explains, 'so that the tested genuineness of your faith—more precious than gold that perishes though it is tested by fire—may be found to result in praise and glory and honour at the revelation of Jesus Christ' (1 Pet. 1:5-7).

Common to all these and other references concerning trials is the concept of 'testing', which is built on the verbal root 'dokimazo', which means to put something through a process of testing so that it is proved to be genuine, fit for purpose and therefore is approved and esteemed. The ultimate test is, of course, God's assessment of our life and work on the day of judgment, but that process is already operative in the present and one of the major marks of proven reality is the Christian's steadfast adherence to hope, in the midst of affliction and trials. The agency may be directly Satanic (as with Job), or godless human beings (as with David) but all that happens is to be seen as under God's sovereign control, under His hand of mercy and grace. The pressures drive the believer to the Lord as the only refuge, the only source of strength, so that just like a metal purified and made stronger by the refiner's fire, the exercise of faith, both in spite of the difficulties but also because of them, tests and approves the reality of the believer's trust in God, which comes through the trial immeasurably stronger. That is indeed a cause for rejoicing.

However, we must never underestimate the importance of the future hope in developing the strength of steadfast stability in the present. The preaching of the future realities of final judgment, of heaven and hell and of the new creation is strangely lacking from many evangelical pulpits, so that our actions are often predicated on short-term results, or what will most readily relieve the present pressures. Evangelistically, Jesus is often represented as the person who can make your life even better than it already is, rather than the only rescuer from sin and death and hell. Moreover, for Christians, our motivation to live in loving obedience to our Lord Jesus and to commit ourselves to sacrificial service will in a large measure be dependent on how much eternity governs our mind-set here in time. The enemy has always tried to present this

as immature escapism for those who cannot cope with life
– 'pie in the sky, when you die'. He is the god of *this* world,
who has a vested interest in persuading those for whom
sensory perception is the only reality, that there is nothing
beyond. As Bertrand Russell famously put it, 'When I die,
I rot'. 'Wrong,' Hebrews 9:27 declares, 'it is appointed for
man to die once, and after that comes judgment.' But we
Christians are often intimidated by the world's mockery
and cynicism and even downplay the importance of the
heavenly perspective. It used often to be said that you
can be so heavenly minded that you're no earthly use. At
one time that might have been true, when retreat into a
spiritual ghetto was signposted as the way to holiness. But
today our problem is likely to be that we have become so
earthly minded that we are of very little use to heaven.

Yet heaven is not only our ultimate 'destination', it is
also the present context of our life in this world. The Lord
Jesus in His resurrection body was 'taken up in glory'
(1 Tim. 3:16) or as the Apostles' Creed expresses it, 'He
ascended into heaven and sits on the right hand of God
the Father Almighty'. This establishes that heaven is a
real location, where Jesus is. That does not mean that we
can fully understand or describe it, but the imagery that
the Bible uses about the Father's house, or the celestial
city, while inevitably containing elements of symbolism
nevertheless concentrates on the idea of a home in which
we belong, while at the same time reminding us that it is
from His heavenly home that Christ the King exercises
His sovereign rule. It is because all authority has been
given to Him in heaven and on earth (Matt. 28:18) that
we can enter into the work of the eternal kingdom now as

we go into all the world to make disciples of all nations. Heaven is where Jesus is and although we cannot see or locate it at present, the New Testament affirms in many places the existence of a reality within space and time, which is more than just a state of being. Christ is seated at the Father's right hand (the position of sovereign rule and authority) in the heavenly places, which means that He is far above every other power or dominion and we have been raised with Him and share already, in a measure, in that divine power, which has put everything under His feet and given Him 'as head over all things to the church' (see Eph. 1:20-23 and 2:6). He is our advocate with the Father (1 John 2:1) who always lives to make intercession for us (Heb. 7:25).

So we live now in the light of eternity, but we already begin to experience the guarantee of our future inheritance through the gift of the Holy Spirit in the here and now. As Paul reminds the Philippians, 'Our citizenship is in heaven, and from it we await a Saviour, the Lord Jesus Christ, who will transform our lowly body to be like his glorious body, by the power that enables him even to subject all things to himself' (Phil. 3:20). That is the perspective on which the whole of our apprenticeship here in this world has to be focussed, because that is how our trials and afflictions will work together for our good. In the very next verse, Paul concludes, 'Therefore, my brothers, whom I love and long for, my joy and crown, stand firm thus in the Lord, my beloved' (Phil. 4:1). Living in the light of 3:20 is what will keep us standing firm in 4:1.

Living as citizens of God's heavenly kingdom in the here and now will inevitably shape the values and determine the priorities of our earthly ministries. Paul never lost sight of that coming Day, of the crown of righteousness and of the necessity of running the race with patient endurance. That is why, at the end, he could affirm, 'I have fought the good fight. I have finished the race. I have kept the faith' (2 Tim. 4:7). There could be no greater accolade than that of finishing the work the Lord had given him to do. That aspiration for our own lives is what will keep us hard-working and diligent, prayerful and dependent, focussed and faithful, as we too long for His appearing.

ABOUT THE PROCLAMATION TRUST

The Proclamation Trust is all about unashamedly preaching and teaching God's Word, the Bible. Our firm conviction is that when God's Word is taught, God's voice is heard, and therefore our entire work is about helping people engage in this life-transforming work.

We have three strands to our ministry:

Firstly we run the Cornhill Training Course which is a three-year, part-time course to train people to handle and communicate God's Word rightly.

Secondly we have a wide portfolio of conferences we run to equip, enthuse and energise senior pastors, assistant pastors, students, ministry wives, women in ministry and church members in the work God has called them to. We also run the Evangelical Ministry Assembly each summer in London which is a gathering of over a thousand church leaders from across the UK and from around the world.

Thirdly we produce an array of resources, of which this book in your hand is one, to assist people in preaching, teaching and understanding the Bible.

For more information please go to www.proctrust.org.uk

TEACHING THE BIBLE SERIES

OLD TESTAMENT

TEACHING NUMBERS – ADRIAN REYNOLDS 978-1-78191-156-3

TEACHING JOSHUA – DOUG JOHNSON 978-1-5271-0335-1

TEACHING 1 SAMUEL – ANDREW REID 978-1-5271-0532-4

TEACHING 1 KINGS – BOB FYALL 978-1-78191-605-6

TEACHING 2 KINGS – BOB FYALL 978-1-5271-0157-9

TEACHING EZRA – ADRIAN REYNOLDS 978-1-78191-752-7

TEACHING RUTH & ESTHER – CHRISTOPHER ASH 978-1-5271-0007-7

TEACHING PSALMS VOL. 1 – CHRISTOPHER ASH 978-1-5271-0004-6

TEACHING PSALMS VOL. 2 – CHRISTOPHER ASH 978-1-5271-0005-3

TEACHING ISAIAH – DAVID JACKMAN 978-1-84550-565-3

TEACHING DANIEL – ROBIN SYDSERFF, BOB FYALL 978-1-84550-457-1

TEACHING AMOS – BOB FYALL 978-1-84550-142-6

NEW TESTAMENT

TEACHING MATTHEW – DAVID JACKMAN, WILLIAM PHILIP
978-1-84550-480-9

TEACHING MARK – ROBIN SYDSERFF 978-1-5271-0533-1

TEACHING ACTS – DAVID COOK 978-1-84550-255-3

TEACHING ROMANS VOL. 1 – CHRISTOPHER ASH 978-1-84550-455-7

TEACHING ROMANS VOL. 2 – CHRISTOPHER ASH 978-1-84550-456-4

TEACHING EPHESIANS – SIMON AUSTEN 978-1-84550-684-1

TEACHING 1 & 2 THESSALONIANS – ANGUS MACLEAY 978-1-78191-325-3

TEACHING 1 TIMOTHY – ANGUS MACLEAY 978-1-84550-808-1

TEACHING 2 TIMOTHY – JONATHAN GRIFFITHS 978-1-78191-389-5

TEACHING JAMES – *MERVYN ELOFF* 978-1-5271-0534-8

TEACHING 1 PETER – ANGUS MACLEAY 978-1-84550-347-5

TEACHING 2 PETER & JUDE – ANGUS MACLEAY 978-1-5271-0563-8

TEACHING 1, 2, 3 JOHN – MERVYN ELOFF 978-1-78191-832-6

PRACTICAL PREACHING

PT RESOURCES

TEACHING
JAMES

From text to message

MERVYN ELOFF

SERIES EDITORS: JON GEMMELL & DAVID JACKMAN

978-1-5271-0534-8

Teaching James

Mervyn Eloff

The letter of James is a much loved epistle in the New Testament. People warm to its seemingly practical nature as it instructs us in the nuts and bolts of the Christian life. However, it is not an easy letter to preach and teach. People struggle to see how the letter fits together and are confused about its overall theme and purpose. This is where Teaching James will prove to be of great assistance. Mervyn Eloff will guide you through the intricate detail of the letter whilst never losing sight of the overall theme and purpose of this dynamic Bible book. A book that is as potent and challenging today as it was when the dispersed Christians read it in the First Century.

Here is a clear, transparent and thorough analysis for preachers – or anyone who wants to work through this Bible book. Years of experience and thoughtful evaluations are distilled into this great resource for anyone preparing to teach through James.

Nat Schluter

Principal, Johannesburg Bible College, Johannesburg, South Africa

Eloff's careful and nuanced work in the text of James makes this an invaluable volume for anyone seeking to preach or teach from this rich letter. Especially useful are the section on the melodic line of the letter and clarity of the theme statements throughout. This is probably the best thing I've read on James.

Robert Kinney

Director of Ministries, Simeon Trust

TEACHING
MARK

From text to message

ROBIN SYDSERFF

SERIES EDITORS: JON GEMMELL & DAVID JACKMAN

978-1-5271-0533-1

Teaching Mark

Robin Sydserff

Mark's gospel is a book that we think we know. It appears straight forward, fast paced and simple. However anyone who has spent any time engrossed in its pages will be aware that under the surface there is great depth and profundity. Robin has written *Teaching Mark* to help the preacher and teacher in the study to not just skim the surface of this life changing account but to go deep and see what is really there.

Robin Sydserff has preached through Mark three times in the last 10 years and taught this material in a variety of other contexts – it shows! He not only has a deep knowledge and love of the text but an infectious passion for the Lord Jesus Christ Himself. Mark's gospel is familiar to many but Teaching Mark *will help any bible study leader or preacher to hear God's voice more clearly and to teach His word more faithfully. It will inspire many to preach Christ and Him crucified from this great gospel!*

Paul Clarke

Senior Minister, St Andrews Free Church, Scotland

TEACHING
2 PETER & JUDE

From text to message

ANGUS MACLEAY

SERIES EDITORS: JON GEMMELL & DAVID JACKMAN

978-1-5271-0563-8

Teaching 2 Peter & Jude

Angus MacLeay

The books of 2 Peter and Jude are some of the least preached in the New Testament. However, these dynamic little books have an important message to be declared to the church in the 21st century. The need to 'contend for the faith' is vital in a confusing church landscape of compromise, pragmatism and drift. These books are dense and brimming with truth and so our hope is that this book helps you see all that is contained within their pages.

Teaching 2 Peter and Jude is a great addition to the growing 'Teaching the Bible' series. It will be a great aid to those who have the privilege and joy of teaching or preaching these particular books. Whether you are a small group leader, preacher, youth worker or someone who simply want help with their personal Bible study, this book will help you to comprehend and communicate the messages of 2 Peter and Jude.

The study embodies exactly the qualities it seeks to enable: humble listening to God's Word, wrestling with the literary structure, big idea, aim, illustration and application, a willingness to contend for the faith, a contending that is biblical in shape, tone and purpose, a fresh focus on the Lord Jesus Christ, a sustained determination to grow in knowledge of Christ, seasoned with wholesome realism about the ever present danger from false teaching. Every preacher will appreciate such prayerful wisdom, and the fruit from decades of preaching that lie behind a book of this quality.

Johnny Juckes
President, Oak Hill College, London

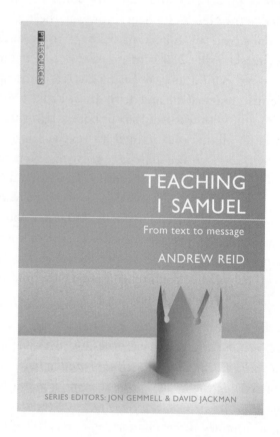

**TEACHING
1 SAMUEL**

From text to message

ANDREW REID

SERIES EDITORS: JON GEMMELL & DAVID JACKMAN

978-1-5271-0532-4

Teaching 1 Samuel

Andrew Reid

The book of 1 Samuel is a blockbuster. One of the most well–known books of the Old Testaments, its gripping narrative is dominated by big characters. Andrew Reid helps preachers get a handle on the vital part it plays in the unfolding story of the Bible.

It is so good to have the fruit of Andrew Reid's study of 1 Samuel now applied to how to be preaching this Old Testament book. Here we have an experienced guide helping us study God's Word carefully: there are no pre-packaged sermons (or Bible studies), but instead you will find yourself motivated to look again at the biblical text more carefully. I think the book is worth reading even for the 'Listening to the Whole of Scripture' sections in each chapter alone.

Neil Watkinson
International Director, Proclamation Trust

Christian Focus Publications

Our mission statement –

STAYING FAITHFUL
In dependence upon God we seek to impact the world through literature faithful to His infallible Word, the Bible. Our aim is to ensure that the Lord Jesus Christ is presented as the only hope to obtain forgiveness of sin, live a useful life and look forward to heaven with Him.

Our books are published in four imprints:

CHRISTIAN
FOCUS

Popular works including biographies, commentaries, basic doctrine and Christian living.

CHRISTIAN
HERITAGE

Books representing some of the best material from the rich heritage of the church.

MENTOR

Books written at a level suitable for Bible College and seminary students, pastors, and other serious readers. The imprint includes commentaries, doctrinal studies, examination of current issues and church history.

CF4•K

Children's books for quality Bible teaching and for all age groups: Sunday school curriculum, puzzle and activity books; personal and family devotional titles, biographies and inspirational stories – because you are never too young to know Jesus!

Christian Focus Publications Ltd,
Geanies House, Fearn, Ross-shire,
IV20 1TW, Scotland, United Kingdom.
www.christianfocus.com
blog.christianfocus.com